DEVEREUX, Eric Gordon
DHU, Lionel Edward
DIEWS, Bernard Albert
DIMMOCK, Donald Charles
DIX, Gordon Kenneth
DIXON, Thomas Charles
DOBSON, Herbert Hartfield
DODDS, Richard
DOXEY, Alexander Harold
DOYLE, Edward Francis
DRAKE, Albert Reginald
DRAKE, John Richardson
DUNCAN, Emmanuel Robert Thomas
DUNDON, Stephen
DUNIN, Thomas
EAGAR, Alexander Vinrace
EDDY, Edwin Ross
EDENBOROUGH, Alan Grosvenor
EDGOOSE, John Franklyn
EDWARDS, Ernest
EDWARDS, Frederick
ELDER, Bruce Alfred
EVANS, Francis Richard
EWENS, Robert Underdown
FAHEY, William Richard
FARRAND, Leonard Charles
FAULKNER, Arthur John
FERGUSON, David Wallace
FERGUSON, Kenneth Charles
FIBBENS, William Sidney
FINDLAY, Gordon Lindsay
FINLAYSON, Harry
FISHER, John William
FITZGERALD, Augustine Francis
FITZGERALD, Lloyd Gerald
FLEMING, Wilfred Stafford
FOOTE, Reginald Eric
FORBES, Robert Gordon Staunton
FORSYTH, Glenbervie Edwin
FORTH, Herbert
FOSTER, Norman Douglas

FOSTER, Roy Ebenezer
FOULKES, Robert Eugene
FRANKLIN, Edward William
FRASER, Noel James
FREER, Walter Edward Albert
FRIAR, Jack Allan
FRISCH, Ernest Dudley
FRITH, William Railton Oliver
FRY, Robert Aubrey
FRYER, Kenneth James
FULLER, John Albert Ernest
GALE, Raymond
GAMBLE, Frank Harold
GAMBLE, Ronald Frederick
GARDINER, Heathcote Diggery
GARNETT, William Henry
GARRETT, Basil Farmer
GENGE, Francis Harrison
GENTLES, Harry Spencer
GILSENAN, Dudley John
GLACKIN, Thomas Nevin
GLASBY, Harold
GOODWIN, Neil Francis
GOODWIN, Wilfred James
GOTHARD, Edwin
GRACO, Henry Mathias
GRAHAM, George Albert
GREAVES, Sidney
GREEN, Arthur Eric
GREEN, John Rex
GREEN, Theo Lawrence
GREENWOOD, James Herbert
GREGSON, Michael Oswald
GRINTER, Norman Francis
GRONBERG, Ernest Edward
GWYNNE, David Andrew
HAAG, Francis Vincent
HAGAN, Allan
HAMMOND, Lawson
HANDCOCK, Richard Daniel
HARE, Richard William

HARRICKS, Sydney William
HARRINGTON, Albert Frederick
HARRIS, Ronald Charles
HARRISON, Leslie Alexander
HARTMANN, Frederick Holland
HASKER, John Reid
HASLAM, Aubrey Cecil
HASS, Mervan Loui Wallace
HATTERSLEY, Jack Osberg
HAWKER, George Clarence
HAWKES, Sydney William
HAYNES, Frank James
HAYWOOD, George James
HEATON, Edmund
HENDERSON, William Laurence Douglas
HENRICKSON, John Olaf
HERINGTON, Henry Foster
HERITAGE, Roy George
HERROD, Herbert Frederick
HEWETT, Edmund Herbert
HICKEY, Robert Arthur
HILL, Douglas Hugh
HILL, Peter
HILL, Robert Henry
HOBBS, George James
HOGAN, Michael Henry
HOLDER, Edward Harrison
HOLM, Clarence Kenneth Asby
HOMARD, Keith
HOMER, Arthur Wilfred
HONOR, Charles Leslie
HOOPER, Edgar Norman
HOPCRAFT, Robert Beauchamp
HORE, Keith Beresford
HORRIGAN, Cornelius
HOUSTON, John Kerr
HOWARD, Leonard John
HUDSON, James Lloyd
HUTCHINSON, Richard
HUTCHINSON, Roy Harold
HUTCHISON, James Robertson

JOHNSON, Percy Albert
JOHNSTON, Donald Erskine
JOHNSTON, Edgar William
JOHNSTON, George
JOHNSTONE, Trevor James Armistice
JONES, David James
JONES, Donald Edgar
JONES, Ivan David
JONES, John Banks
JONES, Philip Trevor
JONES, Wilfred George
JORDAN, Ernest John
JORDAN, Horace David
JOYCE, William Robert John
KEANE, Walter John
KEARNON, Rex Allan
KEENAN, Francis Bernard
KEITH, Andrew Ian
KELLY, James Vincent
KELLY, Neville Andrew
KENNEDY, Robert John
KENNEY, Arthur Henry Lawrence
KENT, Lloyd Shackleton
KETTLE, Edward James
KETTYLE, James Thomas
KEYS, Rodger Francis
KING, Allen James
KIRKHAM, Eric James
KITCHIN, Clayton Peter
KLEINIG, Arthur Albert
KNAPMAN, Wesley Bowden
KNAPP, Douglas John
KNIGHT, Neil Kenneth
KREIG, Archibald Douglas
LAFFER, Peter Morton

HMAS *SYDNEY* (II)

HMAS *SYDNEY* (II)

EDITED BY M. McCARTHY

WESTERN AUSTRALIAN
muSeum

Dr M. McCarthy is a curator in Maritime Archaeology at the Western Australian Museum and leads the museum's HMAS *Sydney*/HSK *Kormoran* research program. He was official observer on board MV *Geosounder* for the Commonwealth Government when the two wrecks were identified.

First Published 2010 by the
Western Australian Museum
49 Kew Street, Welshpool,
Western Australia 6106
(Postal: Locked Bag 49, Welshpool DC. WA 6986)
www.museum.wa.gov.au

Designed by Cathie Glassby.
Back cover: Ship's company, HMAS *Sydney*, Mediterranean, July 1940. Western Australian Museum (Burnsyde-Fox Collection).
Front cover: see page 28.
All background photographs ©iStockphoto.com: endpapers, pp 5, 6, 13, 33, 97, 103, 146, 156 — mikeuk; p. 2 — rustycloud; pp 41, 46–53, 111 — RapidEye; pp 50, 125 — andipantz.
Printed by South Wind Productions, Singapore.

National Library of Australia
Cataloguing-in-publication entry

Author: McCarthy, Michael, 1947–
Title: HMAS Sydney (II) / edited by M. McCarthy.
ISBN: 9781920843496 (pbk.)
Notes: Includes index.
Bibliography.
Subjects: Australia. Royal Australian Navy — History.
World War, 1939-1945 — Naval operations, Australian.
Cruisers (Warships) — Australia — History.
Other Authors/Contributors: Western Australian Museum.
Dewey Number: 940.545994

Australian Government

Department of the Environment, Water, Heritage and the Arts

This publication is generously funded by Maritime Heritage Section, Historic Heritage Branch, Department of the Environment, Water, Heritage and the Arts.

CONTENTS

FOREWORDS

The Hon. Peter Garrett AM MP
Minister for the Environment, Heritage and the Arts

The stories associated with historic shipwrecks in Australian waters provide an insight into Australia's significant maritime heritage. Each shipwreck is a precious record of our past, serving as a marker of significant events in our national story. One such narrative that can only now be fully told follows the finding of the Second World War shipwrecks of HMAS *Sydney* (II) and HSK *Kormoran*.

The loss of *Sydney* with all hands off Western Australia in November 1941 is Australia's single largest naval loss. On that day all of *Sydney*'s 645-strong crew perished following a battle with the German raider *Kormoran,* which itself lost more than 80 sailors.

The story of what really happened to the *Sydney* has been the subject of almost seventy years of intense public interest, involving rumour, speculation, conspiracy theories and hoaxes.

Unsuccessful searches for both shipwrecks and the reliance on the German survivors for eyewitness accounts of the battle contributed to many people being unable to accept the loss and the official version of events.

With the help of funding from the Australian Government both shipwrecks were finally located in March 2008. The findings of the subsequent HMAS *Sydney* (II) Commission of Inquiry into the loss of the *Sydney* largely corroborated the original version of events, supported by new, empirical evidence from the two shipwrecks.

Both sites are now protected under the *Historic Shipwrecks Act 1976.* This ensures that these historically significant vessels and their relics, including their crews' remains, remain safe from damage, disturbance or removal, and the final resting places of these servicemen are respected in perpetuity.

As Minister for Heritage, I commend this book to you as a contribution to the unfolding story of our maritime heritage.

The Hon John Day MLA
Minister for Culture and the Arts

The nation's undivided attention was captured from the moment the search for the HMAS *Sydney* (II) began off the coast of Western Australia.

The mystery surrounding the loss of this ship has provoked debate and speculation lasting almost seven decades.

The search and subsequent location of the wreck sites of both the Australian warship HMAS *Sydney* (II) and the ship that sank her, German raider *HSK Kormoran*, is set to become another fascinating chapter in our state's history.

The Western Australian Museum's publication, *HMAS* Sydney *(II)*, traces the tragic events around what was the largest loss of life ever suffered in a naval battle in the nation's history.

Many dedicated historians, groups, organisations and individuals have never stopped searching for the answers to the riddle of the *Sydney*.

The crew aboard this story's search vessel, the MV *Geosounder*, helped solve one of our country's greatest maritime mysteries — the loss of 654 Australians who perished in unexplained circumstances when the *Sydney* went down off Shark Bay on 19 November 1941.

So many people have been involved in this search over the years — everyone who ever came forward with a letter, a document, a piece of information or an account of what they saw on that fateful day or what they had been told by others who did — you are part of this success story.

The WA Museum's *HMAS* Sydney *(II)* publication covers the history of the ship, its loss and some of the many theories about where and how it might have gone down and why there were no survivors. It also contains accounts of the discovery of the wreck sites, the subsequent Commonwealth Government Inquiry and details the future protection of the sites of both warships.

The real life impact of this famous mystery is brought home in a powerful way in this book through the moving personal stories of some of those who were part of the *Sydney*'s crew.

Through the Western Australian Museum, the State will do its upmost to ensure that the dignity and integrity of the final resting place is honoured and preserved from harm in years to come.

I commend this publication to all those now and in the future who wish to read this clear and moving account of a very special story in our nation's history.

Ms Diana Jones
A/CEO, Western Australian Museum

The Western Australian Museum through its maritime archaeology team has been involved in the search for the HMAS *Sydney* (II) for many years.

The Museum holds a collection of artefacts relating to the ship and its crew and is proud to now also hold, along with the Australian War Memorial, the footage and photographs from the MV *Geosounder*'s successful search for the wreck sites of both the *Sydney* and her adversary, HSK *Kormoran*.

We hope this publication contributes to the documentation of the extraordinary events surrounding the loss of the ship and its crew for present and future generations.

We are proud to hold this responsibility to ensure that this part of the nation's history continues to be documented and told so that the legacy of such a loss will never be forgotten.

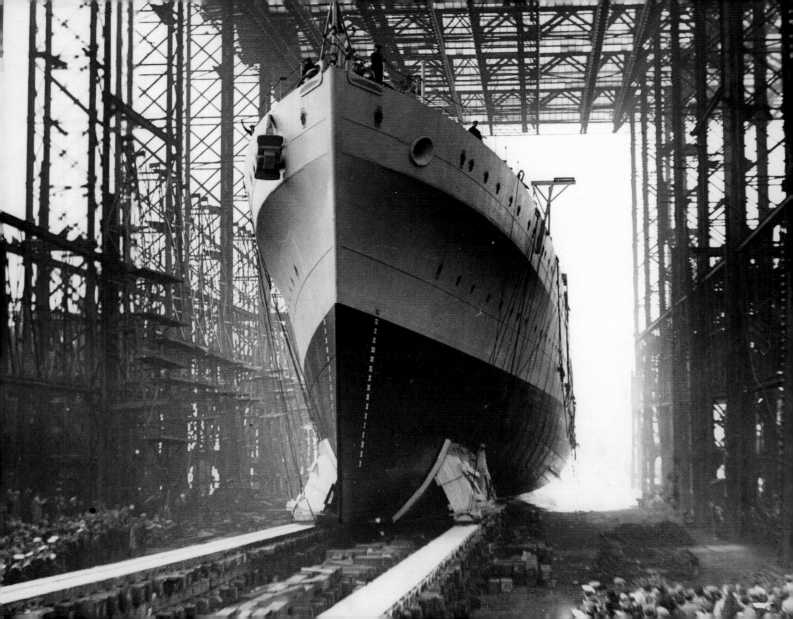

1

HMAS *SYDNEY* (II)
LEGENDARY WARRIOR

---

edited and revised by M. McCarthy

(Sources: Sea Power Centre — Australia, RAN, and *HMAS* Sydney by VADM Sir John Collins KBC CB)[1]

HMAS *Sydney* (II)

After being laid down in 1933 for the Royal Navy as HMS *Phaeton*, HMAS *Sydney* (II) was purchased on the stocks (before launching) by the Australian Government in 1934 and renamed in memory of the earlier HMAS *Sydney* (I) that destroyed the German cruiser SMS *Emden* at the Cocos Keeling Islands in 1914 (see page 16).

HMAS *Sydney* (II) commissioned at Portsmouth on 24 September 1935 under the command of Captain J.U.P. FitzGerald, RN, and spent the early part of her career on the Mediterranean Station taking an active role in the Abyssinian Crisis.

Arriving in Australia on 2 August 1936, *Sydney* remained in home waters until the outbreak of war and was in Fremantle on the day war was declared. On 16 November Captain J.A. Collins, RAN, assumed command from Captain J.W.A. Waller, RN, who had succeeded Captain FitzGerald in 1937.

Sydney remained on local patrol duties until April 1940, when she sailed from Fremantle as part of the escort for a large Middle East-bound convoy. Parting company in the mid-Indian Ocean, the cruiser arrived in Colombo on 8 May 1940.

On 19 May 1940 she proceeded to the Mediterranean and arrived in Alexandria, Egypt, on 26 May, where she joined the 7th Cruiser Squadron of the British Mediterranean Fleet. There *Sydney* experienced her first action when she took part in the bombardment of Bardia on 21 June 1940 in company with British cruisers and destroyers and a French battleship. During this bombardment *Sydney* fired 150 6-inch, high-explosive shells, and her Seagull aircraft, which had been sent to spot

HMAS *SYDNEY* (II) Specifications

HMAS *Sydney* (II).

Sea Power Centre — Australia

Type	Modified Leander-class light cruiser
Laid down	8 July 1933
Launched	22 September 1934
Builder	Swan, Hunter and Wigham Richardson Ltd, Wallsend on Tyne, England
Commissioned	24 September 1935
Displacement	6,830 tons
Length	562 feet 3 inches
Beam	56 feet 8 inches
Armament	8 x 6-inch guns
	4 x 4-inch guns
	12 x 0.5-inch machine guns, in three quad mounts
	12 x .303-inch Lewis guns
	8 x 21-inch torpedo tubes (in two quadruple mounts)
Horsepower	72,000
Speed	32.5 knots
Complement	645

Commanding Officers

Assumed Command	Commanding Officer
24 September 1935	Captain J.U.P. FitzGerald RN
9 October 1937	Captain J.W.A. Waller RN
16 November 1939	Captain J.A. Collins RAN
14 May 1941	Captain J. Burnett RAN

the fall of shell, was attacked by fighters. Damaged and unable to return to the ship, it made a forced landing at an allied airbase, albeit without loss of life.

A week later, in company with other ships of the 7th Cruiser Squadron, *Sydney* encountered three Italian destroyers. The action that followed was fought at dusk in fast-failing light and two of the destroyers succeeded in evading the Allied cruisers. *Sydney*'s role in this action consisted chiefly of finishing off the remaining destroyer *Espero*, which had been crippled in the pursuit, and rescuing 47 Italian survivors.

> " *The odds on paper were two to one against us being able to fight two cruisers ... we had our chance and Buckley's.* "
>
> Lieutenant W.H. Ross[2]

On 1 July 1940 *Sydney* returned to Alexandria where she remained until 7 July, then proceeded as part of the covering force for Malta convoys before joining the Mediterranean Battle Fleet. Following a period of severe air attacks, four of them directed at *Sydney* that were successfully beaten off, she then took part in the first full-scale action with the Italian Fleet: the Battle of Calabria on 9 July.

Three British battleships, one aircraft carrier and four cruisers, including *Sydney* and attendant destroyers, took part against two Italian battleships, 12 cruisers and many destroyers. With the sun behind them, the Italian cruisers opened fire at 1515 hrs. The British cruisers, though outnumbered, engaged the enemy and the British battleship *Warspite* opened fire, hitting the Italian battleship *Giulio Cesare* with a 15-inch shell near her foremost funnel. This caused the Italian fleet to draw rapidly away to the north. By 1611 hrs only one enemy ship remained within range.

At something over 20,000 yards *Sydney* turned her attention to enemy destroyers that were laying smoke to hide their larger ships.[3] Shortly afterwards the British destroyers moved in to attack. By 1640 hrs the engagement was over, although air attacks on the Allied fleet followed. *Sydney* again came through unscathed despite a stick of bombs straddling the ship.

Sydney remained at sea with the Mediterranean Fleet until 13 July 1940, when she returned to Alexandria.

The Battle of Cape Spada

On 18 July 1940, *Sydney* sailed from Alexandria in company with the destroyer HMS *Havock*. Her orders were to support the destroyers *Hyperion*, *Ilex*, *Hero* and *Hasty*, which were engaged in a hunt for enemy submarines off Crete, and to destroy enemy shipping in the Gulf of Athens. The two ships arrived off Crete at sunset and passed through Kaso Strait.

Early on the morning of 19 July *Sydney* and *Havock* reached a point some 40 miles north of Cape Spada. The day had dawned calm and cloudless, with some light fog. At 0733 hrs the cruiser received a report from the destroyer group indicating the presence of two enemy cruisers some 10 miles to the south-west of their position, heading north. On his own initiative, Captain Collins, maintaining radio silence, altered course and proceeded at maximum speed towards the enemy. At 0820 hrs *Sydney* and *Havock* sighted smoke on the horizon. A few minutes later two Italian 6-inch cruisers, the *Bartolomeo Colleoni* and the *Giovanni delle Bande Nere*, were

A 'Sweetheart' badge typical of that given to wives and girlfriends by members of HMAS *Sydney*'s crew.

John Perryman

SMS *Emden* following its battle with
HMAS *Sydney* (I), run aground by its
captain on the North Keeling Island
to avoid loss of the crew. Australian
sailors in the foreground.

Australian War Memorial
Negative Number H18852

World acclamation follows a magnificent naval victory

HMAS SYDNEY's moment of glory was on 19 July, 1940 when she tackled two of the fastest cruisers in the world and sank one.

Her smart gunnery, chasing the much faster and equally heavily armed Italian cruisers, put an end to the BARTOLOMEO COLLEONI.

SYDNEY had joined the British Mediterranean Fleet at Alexandria on 26 May, 1940 after spending the first eight months of the war in Australian waters and the Indian Ocean.

A fortnight later, the Allies were at war with Mussolini's Italy and the SYDNEY was in action with the 7th Cruiser Squadron.

On 21 June, she took part in the bombardment of Bardia and lost her spotter plane, which crash-landed after being attacked by British aircraft which had mistaken it for Italian.

There was plenty of action — bombs, gunfire and torpedoes — in the next three weeks to sharpen up SYDNEY for her engagement with history.

On 18 July, 1940 SYDNEY set sail from Alexandria on a sweep for enemy shipping. She shepherded a group of destroyers — HYPERION, HERO, HASTY and ILEX — for 24 hours, before breaking off to commence her assignment, with a fifth destroyer, HAVOCK, in company.

Only an hour or so after SYDNEY's departure, the HYPERION's captain reported two cruisers — the BARTOLOMEO COLLEONI and the ▶

Back at the Mediterranean post of Alexandria after sinking the BARTOLOMEO COLLEONI, SYDNEY's crew show off the only damage sustained in the battle. (Department of Information)

sighted on the starboard beam at a range of some 23,000 yards, course east-north-east.

At 0829 hrs *Sydney* opened fire with her 6-inch guns on the leading cruiser *Giovanni delle Bande Nere* and both Italian cruisers replied to *Sydney*'s fire. None of the enemy shells scored a hit, though some salvos succeeded in straddling. Within six minutes of opening fire, hits appeared to have been registered on *Giovanni delle Bande Nere*, on whom *Sydney* continued to concentrate her fire. At 0838 hrs *Hyperion*, *Hasty*, *Hero* and *Ilex* were sighted to the south-east at a distance of some six miles. At this time the enemy attempted to escape to the south-west, and by 0846 hrs *Sydney*, with the destroyers in line abreast and in fairly close order, was chasing the enemy at full speed, the destroyers having also opened fire.

With *Giovanni delle Bande Nere* obscured by smoke, *Sydney* shifted her fire to *Bartolomeo Colleoni* at a range of 18,000 yards. At 0851 hrs the two enemy cruisers suddenly altered course to port and soon after appeared to be turning to starboard, eventually coming back to their original south-westerly course, having left a large smokescreen behind them. The Italian cruisers were faster than *Sydney* and were slowly drawing away at approximately 30 knots. At 0902 hrs *Sydney* again opened fire on *Giovanni delle Bande Nere* at 21,000 yards and kept firing until heavy smoke again forced a shift of target to the rearward cruiser.

Sydney's fire on *Bartolomeo Colleoni* appeared to be taking effect and the range had closed to 17,500 yards. Meanwhile both cruisers continued to reply with fairly accurate fire and at 0921 hrs *Sydney* was hit in the foremost funnel. Only one minor casualty resulted. The range was now closing rapidly and at 0923 hrs *Bartolomeo*

Commemorative medal awarded to officers and crew of HMAS *Sydney* after sinking the *Bartolomeo Colleoni*. The obverse carries the legend: *Presented by the citizens of Sydney to Captain J.A. Collins CB, RAN, the officers and ship's company in commemoration of their gallant fight against superior speed and weight of armament, which resulted in the sinking of the Italian Cruiser Bartolomeo Colleoni in the Mediterranean Sea, July Nineteen 1940.*

Western Australian Museum (W.H. [John] Ross Collection)

Colleoni was finally put out of action some five miles off Cape Spada. The surviving cruiser rounded Agria Grabus Island to the north and retired at full speed to the south-west, hotly pursued by *Sydney* almost directly astern.

At 0933 hrs Collins ordered the destroyers to finish off *Bartolomeo Colleoni* with torpedoes and *Sydney* ceased firing soon after, when the range was 7,500 yards. The destroyers *Hyperion* and *Ilex* then fired torpedoes at *Bartolomeo Colleoni*, and the destroyer *Havock* stood by to rescue survivors. *Bartolomeo Colleoni* finally sank at 0959 hrs. Meanwhile *Sydney*, in company with *Hero* and *Hasty*, continued the pursuit of *Giovanni delle Bande Nere*, which had continued to the south at full speed. The fleeing cruiser kept up a desultory, inaccurate fire but *Sydney* stayed in pursuit until 1011 hrs, when the fast-opening range and hazy conditions made overhauling unlikely.

With only 10 rounds of 6-inch shells available to her forward turrets, Collins reluctantly abandoned the chase and was ordered to return to Alexandria to replenish fuel and ammunition. Before reaching Alexandria, *Sydney* and the destroyers were subject to repeated air attacks, with *Havock* sustaining a direct hit. At 11 am on 20 July the triumphant *Sydney*, in company with the British destroyers, reached Alexandria safely, where they were met with rousing cheers from units of the Mediterranean Fleet.

During August *Sydney* took part (as a covering force) in the second bombardment of Bardia. On 4 September, in concert with the destroyer HMS *Ilex*, *Sydney* was ordered to bombard an airstrip at Makri Yalo on the island of Scarpanto. Aware

Troops disembarking the
HMAS *Sydney* at Suda Bay
in Crete, November 1940.

Sea Power Centre — Australia

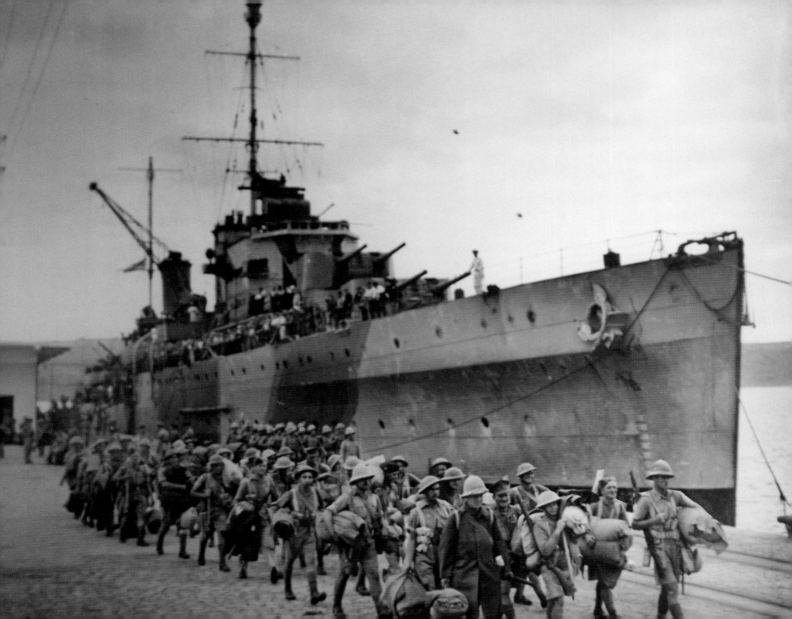

that there might be strong harbour defences, including high-speed torpedo boats (E-boats), Collins decided to disguise *Sydney* as an Italian Condottiere-class cruiser and to make an approach to a nearby harbour under that disguise until well within firing range. Using wooden frames and canvas to change the shape of the ship's funnel, the ruse proved successful. The E-boats on patrol were initially unsuspecting, and as *Sydney* opened fire on the airstrip *Ilex* proceeded to sink two E-boats before the rest made off. The attack was a great success and the two allied ships, including *Sydney's* aircraft, which had been flown off before dawn to spot the fall of shell, departed unscathed and returned safely to the fleet despite a number of air attacks.[5]

> *" ... a huge cloud of mixed black and white smoke, then the glorious warship ... heeled over to port and sank. "*
>
> Admiral Casardi on the loss of *Bartolomeo Colleoni*[4]

Sydney docked in Alexandria on 8 September, remaining there until 24 September 1940. In October she was again operating with the Mediterranean Fleet, taking part in a sweep of the Adriatic and in protecting convoys to Greece.

On 11 November the Mediterranean Fleet successfully launched an attack by carrier aircraft on the Italian Fleet, which was concentrated in the port of Taranto. In support of this operation, *Sydney* was engaged in operations in the Straits of Otranto when an Italian convoy was successfully attacked during the hours of darkness on the night of 12–13 November. December 1940 saw *Sydney* again covering convoys to Greece and Malta, and participating in further operations in the Adriatic and Straits of Otranto as part of the Mediterranean Fleet. On 23 December 1940 she put into Malta for a refit, sailing again on 8 January 1941.

Return to Australian waters

In January 1941 *Sydney* sailed from Alexandria for Australia, reaching Fremantle on 5 February where she received a hero's welcome. Her arrival in her namesake city on 10 February saw her crew feted with a civic reception and school children given a public holiday so they could see her and her valiant crew as they paraded through the city. A refit at Garden Island in Sydney followed, after which *Sydney* took up patrol-and-convoy escort duties off the Australian coast under the command of Captain Joseph Burnett, RAN. In April 1941 she paid a brief visit to Singapore, and later in the year visited Noumea, Auckland and Suva in her role as convoy escort before returning to Western Australian waters.

PAGE 27

Sydney crew members standing in a hole in the forward funnel sustained in action against the *Bartolomeo Colleoni*, Alexandria, 1940

Australian War Memorial Negative Number 002435

"The most beautiful and serene sight was when I used to race over to the train bridge and watch that wonderful ship sailing into the harbour. Then I would race to Victoria Quay where it would always berth.

"When the ship sailed for the last time on 11 November 1941 I watched it sail out past Rottnest Island until it was out of sight. When he died, a part of me went with him …

"The only mystery is where it finally rests. I hope the *Sydney* is found …"

THELMA GALE
SISTER OF ABLE SEAMAN GUNNER KENNETH GEORGE TAYLOR

2

TRAGIC VICTORY
HMAS *SYDNEY* IS LOST

edited by M. McCarthy

(Source: Sea Power Centre — Australia, RAN)[6]

Loss of HMAS *Sydney*

HMAS *Sydney* sailed from her berth at Victoria Quay, Fremantle, on Armistice Day, 11 November 1941, to escort the troopship *Zealandia* to Sunda Strait, where she was to be relieved by the British cruiser HMS *Durban* for the last leg of the voyage to Singapore. Though *Zealandia* was thirteen days behind schedule due to industrial trouble, the voyage itself was without incident, and at noon on 17 November *Zealandia* was turned over to *Durban*. *Sydney* then proceeded to Fremantle where she was expected to arrive on the afternoon of 20 November 1941. She did not arrive as expected, and at 11 am the following day the District Naval Officer, Western Australia, reported to the Naval Board that *Sydney* was overdue. This did not immediately concern the Naval Board, which had been advised that *Zealandia* had also arrived later than anticipated, and it was assumed that *Sydney* too had been delayed. There was also the possibility that she might have been diverted for another purpose and was maintaining radio silence. When, however, she had not returned by 23 November she was instructed by the Naval Board to report by signal. There was no reply.

The following account of *Sydney's* final action and subsequent loss is based the Royal Australian Navy's Sea Power Centre's reconstruction of events leading up to *Sydney's* disappearance. It relies on information gathered from interrogations of German survivors from the raider HSK *Kormoran*, which *Sydney* engaged on the afternoon of 19 November 1941, as well as on surviving records.

Returning from her convoy duties to Java, *Sydney* was proceeding south along the north-west coast of Western Australia when she sighted what appeared to be a merchant vessel at about 1700 hrs (Western Australian time) on 19 November 1941, some 120 nautical miles west of Shark Bay.

The ship was in fact the German raider HSK *Kormoran* (commanded by Fregattenkapitän Theodor Anton Detmers), disguised as the Dutch merchantman *Straat Malakka*. *Sydney* challenged the vessel, continuously using her signal lamp while at the same time closing the range between the two ships. Merchant vessels were known to be less efficient at visual signalling, and the Germans exploited this knowledge through their actions on their flag deck and by their slow response to *Sydney*'s challenges.

With Detmers claiming his vessel was the Dutch cargo ship *Straat Malakka*, *Sydney* signalled, both by flags and flashing light: 'Where bound?' Detmers replied: 'Batavia.' *Sydney*'s efforts to

> " *The loss of HMAS* Sydney *with all hands on 19 November 1941 accounted for more than 35% of Royal Australian Navy servicemen killed in action between 1939 and 1945.* "
>
> Richard Summerell[7]

establish the true identity of the vessel resulted in her closing the range to a point where she no longer had the advantage of her superior armament. At 1800 hrs *Kormoran* broadcast a QQQQ 'suspicious ship' message, feigning a cry for help in the name of *Straat Malakka*, and *Sydney* approached from astern with her main armament and torpedo tubes bearing, her aircraft on the catapult with its engine running. By 1815 hrs *Sydney* had drawn almost abeam of *Kormoran* to starboard, soon closing less than a mile distant. Both ships were steering west-south-west at about 14 knots. At around 1825 the aircraft engine was shut down.

The crucial moment then came when *Sydney* hoisted a two-flag signal consisting of the letters 'IK', which the raider could not interpret. They were in fact the two centre letters of the *Straat Malakka*'s four-letter secret identification signal 'IIKP'. With no reply forthcoming *Sydney* signalled in plain language: 'Show your secret sign.'

Finally, when concealment of his vessel's true identity was no longer possible, and with the advantage of surprise, Detmers ordered the Dutch colours to be struck, hoisted the German naval ensign and opened fire with all armament at approximately 1830 hrs.

Sydney's own guns opened fire almost simultaneously with a full salvo that apparently passed over *Kormoran* without inflicting damage. It is likely that the raider's opening fire destroyed *Sydney*'s bridge and director control tower, with the result that the ability to fire her main armament in centrally controlled salvos was immediately negated. *Kormoran* then scored further hits on *Sydney*, again hitting her bridge and midships section. According to the Germans, all of *Kormoran*'s available armament was brought to bear on *Sydney*, concentrating on her bridge, torpedo tubes and anti-aircraft batteries.

For a few seconds after her initial salvo, *Sydney* did not reply. It appears that her forward A and B turrets were put out of action, leaving only her after turrets X and Y to respond individually in local control. It was reported by the Germans that *Sydney*'s X turret opened fast and accurate fire, hitting *Kormoran* in the funnel and engine room. Y turret is said to have fired two or three salvos, all of which went over.

HSK *Kormoran* taking on stores in Kiel Harbour, Germany.

Sea Power Centre — Australia

HSK *KORMORAN* Specifications

Type	Auxiliary raider G, ship 41 *Kormoran* (formerly Hamburg-America Line ship *Steiermark*)
Displacement	8,736 tons
Length	515 feet
Beam	66 feet
Builder	Kiel Shipyards
Speed	18 knots
Armament	6 x 15-cm (5.9-inch) guns. Range 18, 100 yards
	5 x 2-cm anti-aircraft guns
	2 x 3.7-cm anti-aircraft guns
	6 x 21-inch torpedo tubes (2 below the waterline)
	Capable of carrying approximately 360 mines
Aircraft	2 x Arado 196 floatplanes stowed in No 5 hold
Complement	400

At about this time the raider fired two torpedoes at *Sydney*, one of which struck her slightly forward of A turret. The other passed close ahead of the stricken ship, which then turned to port exposing her starboard side to further fire.

With her bow low in the water, *Sydney* continued her turn towards *Kormoran* as though attempting to ram. As she did so, the top of B turret was blown off and flew overboard. The cruiser then passed close under *Kormoran*'s stern, heading southward and losing way. *Kormoran*, maintaining her course and speed, was now on fire in the engine room, where hits by *Sydney*'s X turret had caused a fuel leak and an intense fire. Smoke then hid *Sydney* from *Kormoran*'s bridge but the raider continued to engage with her after guns as the range opened to approximately 4,400 yards.

At about 1845 hrs *Sydney* was observed to fire torpedoes (some Germans thought as many as four). Detmers was attempting to turn to port to bring his broadside to bear when *Kormoran*'s engines began to fail. The torpedo tracks were sighted, but *Kormoran* cleared them and they passed astern before the raider's engines broke down completely.

Sydney, crippled and on fire from the bridge to the after funnel, steamed slowly to the south, returning only sporadic fire from her secondary armament. Although by now the range had opened to 6,600 yards, she continued to receive steady hits from *Kormoran*'s port broadside. At a range of 7,700 yards, *Kormoran* then fired one torpedo that missed *Sydney*'s stern. Although this fierce action had lasted only half an hour, both ships had been dealt mortal blows.

Kormoran fired her last shot at 1925 hrs at a range of about 11,000 yards. It

NAVAL SECTION

Intelligence Memorandum No.76

ACTION REPORT OF ACTION BETWEEN

GERMAN RAIDER 'KORMORAN' AND H.M.A.S. SYDNEY

Translation of German document PG/11875/NID.

Provenance: Ex 'Kormoran' via Frumel.

CYPHER, IN GERMAN, USED BY CAPTAIN DIETMAR

System is multiple alphabetic substitution using fifteen alphabets. All 26 letters plus A B C D are used.

In the substituion table, the normal alphabetic order is used, Z being followed by A B C D.

To construct the Table write this alphabet vertically to the left hand side, and against D (i.e. the last line) write the key word "GEFECHTSBERICHT". The table can now be completed by writing in the fifteen alphabets, all in normal order with the relative position of each being determined by making the appropriate letters correspond with those of the key word.

The message is decyphered by counting from the start of every paragraph sign (⌐/¬); the first letter being in alphabet 1, the second in 2, and so on.

Dots, or full stops, are not counted, their purpose being merely to separate words. The exception is on page 1, paras. 2 and 3 where the groups of 4 dots indicate 4 blanks.

There is a substituion table for numerals. It would appear to be:

A	1	D	4	H	7	D Ø
B	2	E	5	I	8	
C	3	F	6	J	9	

X is used for 'period'

External Distribution

Op-20-G
Frumel
Cdr. (I.C.)

Internal Distribution

Director General
Director
I.E.
I.S.O.
VI
VIII

The dictionary into which Captain Dehmers encoded an action report. (Part of one page only)

Above is enlarged, the left is slightly smaller than actual book.

First Salvo, Ross Shardlow, oil on canvas. The painting shows HMAS *Sydney* under fire. X and Y turrets engaging.

Ross Shardlow

A Carley float from HMAS *Sydney* similar to that which landed at Christmas Island. It is now on exhibition in the Australian War Memorial. Errors in the newspaper account include the date of recovery.

Daily Mirror *(Sydney)*, *Western Australian Museum Collection*

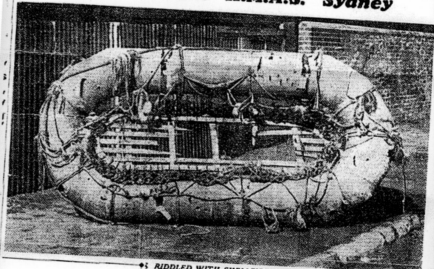

THE DAILY MIRROR, THURSDAY, MARCH 11, 1943.

WIDE OCEAN SWEEP

orth

Relic From The Last Fight Of Gallant H.M.A.S. Sydney

RIDDLED WITH SHELLFIRE, battered from 18 months in the sea, this Carley float from H.M.A.S. Sydney has been washed up on the coast of Western Australia. It is some 18 months since the gallant Sydney, blazing fiercely, staggered away over the horizon after her last fight with a German raider. The curtain then fell, and no more was heard or found of Australia's best known fighting ship. The woodwork of the float is smashed and the cork floats and metal compartments bear the marks of shellfire. It has been handed to Mr. Bryce Farmer, N.S.W. representative of the Australian War Memorial at Canberra.

was claimed by Detmers that *Kormoran* fired as many as 450 rounds from her main armament and hundreds more from her secondary armament. With the gathering gloom, *Sydney* disappeared from view and was last seen by the Germans about ten miles off, heading approximately south-south-east. Thereafter, until about 2300 hrs all that was seen was a distant glare, then occasional flickerings, until midnight, at which time all trace of *Sydney* disappeared.

Of *Sydney*'s total complement of 645 officers and men, none survived. The only material evidence known to have been recovered from *Sydney* at the time was an Australian naval-type Carley life raft recovered eight days after the action by HMAS *Heros*, and an Australian naval-pattern lifebelt recovered by HMAS *Wyrallah*. The Carley float is now preserved in the Australian War Memorial in Canberra.

In February of the following year, a naval Carley float containing a corpse dressed in a boiler suit drifted to Christmas Island and was taken ashore at Flying Fish Cove. The serviceman was not identified. The 'Unknown Sailor' was buried with full military honours, and though an investigation in 1949 concluded he was not from *Sydney*, after his grave was found in 2006 and the body exhumed and subjected to modern forensic analyses, this finding was overturned (see Commission of Inquiry following).

Kormoran survivors

With the situation hopeless due to raging fires within his ship, Detmers gave the order to abandon ship and the first wave of boats left *Kormoran* between 2000 and 2100 hrs.

At that time all accessible lifesaving equipment in the fire-free portion of the ship was put overboard. During this phase a large rubber boat carrying many of the German wounded was overturned, throwing some 40 men into the sea. Only two survived.[8] Almost all the officers and enough ratings to man the guns (around 120 men) waited on board while scuttling arrangements were made. Remaining lifesaving equipment consisted of two steel boats located forward in number two hold, but loss of power on board *Kormoran* required them to be raised by hand, delaying their launch.

At midnight, with smoke increasingly heavy on the mine deck, the scuttling charge was set and the last boat cast off. Half an hour later the charge detonated and the more than 300 mines carried by *Kormoran* exploded and she sank rapidly, stern first.

At 1700 hrs (Western Australian time) on 24 November 1941 the British tanker *Trocas*, bound Palembang for Fremantle, reported by wireless telegraph (W/T) the rescue of 25 German seamen from a raft sighted some 115 miles west-north-west of Carnarvon. This was the first positive evidence of a possible naval engagement involving the overdue *Sydney*. Naval authorities immediately dispatched Royal Australian Navy (RAN) auxiliary craft with armed guards on board to rendezvous with *Trocas*. At the time of receipt of the signal from *Trocas*, air searches seeking *Sydney* were already in progress.

Unbeknown to the naval authorities, the transport *Aquitania* had also sighted a raft and rescued 26 Germans the previous day (23 November). Maintaining W/T silence, her command passed on no information of this until 27 November, when she informed the signal station at Wilsons Promontory in Victoria of her discovery.

Officers and crew from Commander Detmers' lifeboat alongside SS *Centaur*.

Battye Library (5545B/7)

Kapitänleutnant Henry Meyer's lifeboat on the beach at Red Bluff.

Western Australian Museum (donated by Gordon Ewers)

One of Henry Meyer's family photographs. On the reverse of each photograph Meyer, the *Kormoran*'s navigator, kept a log of the lifeboat voyage.

Western Australian Museum (donated by the Meyer family)

KAPITÄNLEUTNANT MEYER'S LOG

19.11   24h Detonat. 19.11 midnight explosion

20.11.   0600 meeting with von Gosseln and one rubber boat. 1200 course NE, 3 sea miles.

21.11   Course ENE. Wind south force 4. Day's run 24 sea miles. Total distance 27 sea miles.

22.11   Course ENE. Wind S to E and S to W. Day's run 36 sea miles. Total distance 63 sea miles. 1800 sea anchor out.

21.11   Evening stormy from the south. Big swell from the SE and SW. Running before the wind the whole night.

22.11   0400 NNE and N with storm foresail then steered NW about 3 sea miles. Wind SSW, S and SE from 0700. 40 degrees 5 sea miles.

1200 Day's run 19 sea miles. Total distance 58 sea miles. From 1200 steered 50 degrees with foresail, at times with mainsail farther to the ENE at 2 knots.

At night the boat takes on a lot of water and we drift.

23.11   Day's run 18 sea miles. Course NE. Total distance 81 sea miles.

0400 Foresail set. Wind SW force 4/5/6. Big sea. SW swell.

24.11   Course ENE. 2.5 knots, evening 1.5 knots. 1200 sighted high, steep coast from about 15 sea miles. Keep going until midnight. Marked time [stopped and held position].

Sailed during the night with foresail. 0700 set the mainsail. From 0800 making 4 knots. SE wind. Big sea until 0700, from 0700 moderate. Day's run 30 + 10. 40 sea miles. Total distance 121 sea miles.

25.11   0330 Seek under foresail a place to land. First bay is a good place but not reachable any more. Second bay all unsuitable. Third bay still to the north as there is no possibility of travelling south either under sail or with oars.

Set watch 1 hour forward. On watch 1st and 2nd division Oberleutnant Schaefer. At 1600 police come and advise that we will be transported to Carnarvon. For 1700. We are driven off in two trucks. At 1900 encountered 48 men from battery 4. Kohls [maybe Kohn or Kuhl] was also there. The drive to Carnarvon was horrible for me. The splinter [Meyer was injured by shrapnel in the battle] appears to be festering. I'm glad that I got the boat here.

Translation by David Kennedy

Cover memo of report of interrogation of *Kormoran* survivors, December 1941.

Australian National Archives (MP1049/5, 2026/19/6)

0/19/18

S e c r e t :

From : D.N.O. FOR W.A.

To : Secretary, Naval Board, MELBOURNE.

FREMANTLE, W. A.
12th December, 1941.

INTERROGATION OF SURVIVORS ex GERMAN
RAIDER 41 - KORMORAN :

Submitted for the information of the Naval Board the attached copies (3) of summary of deductions from interrogation of survivors ex "KORMORAN".

2. With exception of two prisoners, REIMANN and JENTSCH, all have been interrogated. The above two are in hospital for amputation operations.

3. The completed statements of all prisoners interrogated will be forwarded within a few days.

Captain, R.A.N.
DISTRICT NAVAL OFFICER, W.A.

HKS *Kormoran* officers, Dhurringile, February 1943.

Australian War Memorial Negative Number 30185/05

The air searches produced their first results early on the morning of 25 November. At 0700 hrs a lifeboat was sighted north-north-west of Carnarvon. Further sightings during the day revealed up to five boats in the area at that time.

Two boats came ashore unaided on Quobba Station at the 17 Mile Well and Red Bluff some 50 to 60 miles by rough track north of Carnarvon. Alerted by stockman Ahmat Doo to their presence, Keith Baston, the station manager, informed the authorities and land parties were dispatched to apprehend these groups during the afternoon of their landing. The steamer *Koolinda* picked up a third boat, *Centaur* picked up one (containing Detmers) and HMAS *Yandra* another. Based on records made at the time and further research conducted by Barbara Poniewierski, the total number of *Kormoran* survivors rescued was as follows:

Stoker Bill Burnsyde.
The photograph on the right is inscribed 'To Madge with love'.

Western Australian Museum (Burnsyde-Fox Collection)

Trocas	1 rubber raft	25	Landed Fremantle
Aquitania	1 rubber raft	26	Landed Sydney
Centaur	1 life boat	61	Landed Fremantle*
Koolinda	1 life boat	31	Landed Fremantle
Yandra	1 life boat	72	Landed Fremantle
Landed north of Carnarvon	1 life boat	57	
Landed north of Carnarvon	1 life boat	46	

Total of 318 survivors
(315 Germans and three Chinese. The Chinese had been taken from captured ships to work on the *Kormoran*. There was one in the *Centaur* boat, and two in the *Yandra* boat.[9])

* *Centaur* called at Carnarvon, but did not land prisoners there, except for Commander Detmers and First Officer Foerster, who were taken to Fremantle by road.

43

"Bill was still at school when our mother passed away 25 May 1933. I came home to care for the family …
Bill joined the *Sydney* as an able seaman, and had celebrated his twenty-first birthday just two months before the *Sydney* went missing.

"He came to Donnybrook to see me in hospital for my first babe. She was born on 13 November 1941. I was told the evening before I left hospital that the *Sydney* and all hands were missing. It came as a shock to us all.
Bill was almost like a son to me. God rest his soul and all hands from the *Sydney*."

SOPHIE JEFFERY
SISTER OF STOKER WILLIAM EDMUND BURNSYDE

Stoker Jack Crowle.

Glenys McDonald Collection (donated by Crowle family)

To Mum,

Although I know it will be a blow to you, I don't want you to grieve, as I have finished my time on earth and have gone to a better place. You will disappoint me greatly if you do not carry on. My death would not mean that your struggle and sacrifices have been in vain, it just means that your sacrifice was as great as mine. However great this sacrifice is, remember I lived and died an Australian and I don't think there is any greater honour. I am not afraid of death, and would prefer to die in no other way than in doing my duty.

Jack Crowle

Jack Crowle's letter to his mother in case he was lost at sea.

Glenys McDonald Collection (donated by Crowle family)

BUCKINGHAM PALACE

The Queen and I offer you
our heartfelt sympathy in your
great sorrow.

We pray that your country's
gratitude for a life so nobly
given in its service may bring
you some measure of consolation.

George R.I.

Western Australian Museum (Burnsyde-Fox Collection)

Acting Engine Room Artificer
4th Class Alf Shepherd.

*Glenys McDonald Collection
(donated by Margaret Bourne)*

Able Seaman Richard (Dick) Severn Perryman.

Glenys McDonald Collection (donated by the Perryman family)

Steward Ernest David Rolley and his letter of
thanks to Nancy Francis.

Western Australian Museum
(photo donated by the Rolley Family: letter by Ros. Fielding)

9/std T Rolley
Mess 35
H.M.A.S. Sydney
c/o G.P.O.

Dear Miss Francis,

I would like you to thank
the Womens Auxiliary R.S.S.I.L.A for the Postal
Note which I received last time in harbour
although the Period was very short. I hope the
next Port has longer leave as this trip has
been rather long. There is one thing about
the navy one gets quite a change in temperature.
Last week it was bitter cold and miserable
this week it is just the opposite one can't get
cool.

At the moment the Indian Ocean
has seen quite a bit of us or else it is the
other way round but so long as we are on top
is all that we worry about. At the moment we
are waiting for a enemy ship to show up so
we can sink it, but I am afraid they take
some finding.

Well I am afraid there is little
to tell as writing letters at sea are very hard so
I will close with

Kind Regards to all
Yours Sincerely Dave Rolley

P.S. By the way we were Unlucky enough to have spent Easter at sea.

48

O/std D Rolley
Mess 35
HMAS Sydney
c/- G.P.O.

Dear Miss Francis,

I would like you to thank the Women's Auxiliary R.S.S.I.L.A. for the Postal Note which I received last time in harbour although the period was very short. I hope the next Port has longer leave as this trip has been rather long. There is one thing about the navy one gets quite a change in temperature. Last week it was bitter cold and miserable this week it is just the opposite one can't get cool.

At the moment the Indian Ocean has seen quite a bit of us or else it is the other way round but so long as we are on top is all that we worry about. At the moment we are waiting for a enemy ship to show up so as we can sink it, but I am afraid they take some finding.

Well I am afraid there is little to tell as writing letters at sea are very hard so I will close with

Kind Regards to all
Yours sincerely
Dave Rolley

P.S. By the way we were unlucky enough to have spent Easter at sea.

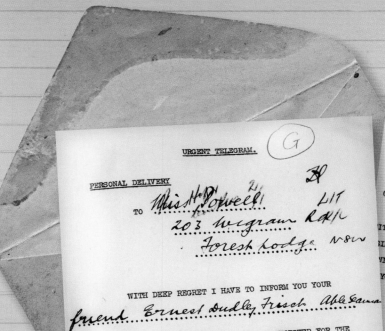

URGENT TELEGRAM.   (G)

PERSONAL DELIVERY

TO *Miss H.B.* 21 3B

203 Wigram Rd/R LIT

Forest Lodge N.S.W.

WITH DEEP REGRET I HAVE TO INFORM YOUR

friend Ernest Dudley Frisch Able Seaman

IS MISSING AS RESULT OF ENEMY ACTION.   MINISTER FOR THE

NAVY AND THE NAVAL BOARD DESIRE TO EXPRESS TO YOU THEIR

SINCERE SYMPATHY.

NAVY.

TYPED

NAVY OFFICE.

BC/EOC.

COPY OF MESSAGE.

To MRS. MARY E. OGILVIE. 59 EVALINE STREET CAMPSIE N.S.W.

From........N.B.

URGENT TELEGRAM PERSONAL DELIVERY/L
Method of Transmission........LIT........CODE.
........CONF. CODE.
........CYP.........PL.

Date and Time Sent........28/11/'41.

Date and Time Received................

Originator's Number................Time of Origin................

WITH DEEP REGRET I HAVE TO INFORM YOU YOUR HUSBAND LAURENCE
OGILVIE. ABLE SEAMAN IS MISSING AS RESULT OF ENEMY ACTION.
MINISTER FOR THE NAVY AND THE NAVAL BOARD DESIRE TO EXPRESS
YOU THEIR SINCERE SYMPATHY.

Copies of advice to family and friends of crew of
HMAS *Sydney* (II) that they are missing.

Sea Power Centre — Australia

Able Seaman Denis Sutton and his wife.

Glenys McDonald Collection (donated by former shipmate Jim Lavender)

Able Seaman Anthony Arthur Bodman.

Western Australian Museum
(donated by Elizabeth Goodwin)

Telegram sent to Patrica Smith, wife of
Able Seaman William Frederick Albert Smith.

Western Australian Museum (donated by Maree Jenssen)

ORNAMENTAL telegram forms
are available for
BIRTHDAY, EASTER & MOTHERS DAY
greetings.
CONGRATULATORY & SOCIAL messages,
as well as
CHRISTMAS & NEW YEAR GREETINGS
—WITHOUT EXTRA CHARGE—

URGENT TELEGRAM

FOR QUICK SERVICE, REPLY BY TELEGRAM.

T.G. 42A.   COMMONWEALTH OF AUSTRALIA—POSTMASTER-GENERAL'S DEPARTMENT.

Funds may be Quickly, Safely and
Economically Transferred by
MONEY ORDER TELEGRAM
(PLEASE TURN OVER)
Sch. C 2941 - 9/1940.

URGENT TELEGRAM

This Telegram has been received subject to the Post
and Telegraph Act and Regulations. The time received
at this office is shown at the end of the message.

The date stamp indicates
the date of reception and
lodgment also, unless an
earlier date is shown after
the time of lodgment

Office of Origin   No. of Words   Time of Lodgment

MELBOURNE 55 6P
POSTAL ACKNOWLEDGMENT DELIVERY PERSONAL ——
MRS PATRICIA M SMITH   O 1734
86 GLADSTONE ST KEW VIC
WITH DEEP REGRET I HAVE TO INFORM YOU YOUR HUSBAND WILLIAM
FREDERICK ALBERT SMITH ABLE SEAMAN IS MISSING AS A RESULT OF
ENEMY ACTION STOP MINISTER FOR THE NAVY AND THE NAVAL BOARD
DESIRE TO EXPRESS TO YOU THEIR SINCERE SYMPATHY ——
                                                    NAVY

7-30P JP

GVI RI

This scroll commemorates
Able Seaman E. G. Baverstock
Royal Australian Navy

held in honour as one who
served King and Country in
the world war of 1939-1945
and gave his life to save
mankind from tyranny. May
his sacrifice help to bring
the peace and freedom for
which he died.

The commemorative scroll sent to the parents
of Able Seaman Edward George Baverstock.

*Western Australian Museum
(donated by Garry Baverstock AM)*

3

THE VACUUM IS FILLED
THEORIES AND SPECULATION

M. McCarthy

(Source: 'An insight into the genesis and evolution of the HMAS *Sydney* controversy.')[10]

The wartime conspiracies

Conspiracy theories and speculation were to be expected in the HMAS *Sydney* case, for when it disappeared a large cross-section of the Australian populace proved unable to accept the German account of its loss. During the war speculation was rife, rumours were endemic and accusations soon came to be levelled at both the German crew and Australian officialdom.

It began at the highest levels when, just five days after the disappearance, Rear Admiral Crace, the senior naval officer in Australia, wrote in his personal diary that the Naval Board thought that a Vichy French submarine might have been involved. Rumours, including the belief that there were two ships involved in sinking *Sydney*, spread rapidly. In noting that they were widespread — one lady was heard talking about the disappearance on a Sydney tram — the Advisory War Council, including the prime minister, chiefs of staff and senior politicians, debated whether to admit that the men were missing. The delay in making an official announcement made matters worse.

Questions surrounding the whereabouts of *Sydney* were also widespread. Some thought that while she was last seen heading toward the south-east, away from the battle, there was a possibility that *Sydney* might have proceeded towards the coast before eventually succumbing. Others thought she might have turned back north and was headed to the nearest dry dock, at either Singapore or Sourabaya. Alternately, some thought she had sunk near the *Kormoran*. In one series of naval signals from late November, the belief was expressed that the German Raider had

PAGE 54

HMAS *Sydney*'s starboard gun crew closed up on mount S1 in late 1940.

Sea Power Centre — Australia

sunk at 26°S 111°E and that *Sydney* was last seen heading south at five knots. In another, it was 'assumed' that *Sydney* had sunk at 26°31'S 111°E. These signals were based on information provided by the German survivors in late November 1941.[11]

Later there were also concerns that the survivors from the crew of *Sydney* had been picked up by enemy ships. Then there were people in Geraldton and elsewhere who thought they had heard signals from the stricken ship. Matters were made worse when a newspaper account, albeit from an unreliable source, appeared in January 1942 indicating that *Kormoran* sank *Sydney* with torpedoes after most of the German crew had abandoned ship and some were rowing towards the victorious *Sydney*. Then in one propaganda broadcast early in the new year, Radio Tokyo claimed that the crew of *Sydney* were prisoners in Japan. This was repeated by Chinese radio. There were also wartime rumours that the cruiser had been seen at anchor during Lieutenant Colonel Doolittle's daring bomber raid on Tokyo in April 1942. Many service personnel believed these stories. The Australian press, believing they were being kept in the dark, called for a full account.

Concerns about the Japanese POW story remained, and in October 1945 Commodore John Collins, the former captain of *Sydney* in the Mediterranean campaign, was directed to ascertain if any information regarding the fate of the ship could be gleaned from Japanese sources. While he found that there was no substance to it at all, the fact that he embarked on this exercise is some indication of the prevailing concerns. Finally, in that same month and despite urgings from RAN staff at Fremantle, Commander Rupert Long, director of Naval Intelligence, refused to publish an account compiled by local RAN staff on the basis that the analysis would still not be accepted by some people as being absolute confirmation of the loss of all crew. He then stated that 'it is intended not to publish anything further concerning this action, and its results, unless the board is forced by ministerial pressure' (see page 125).[12] Although there was continuing disquiet in parliament, and although letters appeared to and from politicians expressing concern and urging further investigation, there the matter ended as far as the authorities were concerned.

The controversies and conspiracies in the 1970s

German-speaking Jonathan Robotham was a former POW in Germany during World War I, and in World War II he was a guard escorting the *Kormoran* survivors on their voyage from Carnarvon down to Fremantle. He later became an intelligence officer at their prison in the eastern states. Convinced that something was wrong with the existing accounts, his became an obsessive post-war quest to find a film and a camera said to have been buried where two lifeboats from *Kormoran* had landed on Quobba Station. While the contents of the lifeboats were retrieved by the authorities, the film and camera were never found.

Although some had never met him, Robotham's beliefs were shared by a number of researchers, some former servicemen, who claimed that they had actually seen record of signals from *Sydney*. They formed the Perth-based Sydney Research Group, which became the font of conspiracy theories alongside Robotham. Partly driven by a belief that the *Kormoran* had surrendered and that a submarine was involved in the sinking, Robotham was also writing a book detailing these claims

VMH/JH

NAVY OFFICE.

COPY OF MESSAGE.

To H.M.S. "ACHILLES" H.M.S. "LEANDER" RESIDENT NAVAL OFFICER SUVA

From S.O. (1) WELLINGTON

Method of Transmission W.T. {P/L. CODE. CONF. CODE. CYP. N. CYPHER A.

Date and Time Sent 28/11/41

Date and Time Received 29/11/41

Originator's Number   Time of Origin 0532Z/28

4077

ECRET. PACIFIC RAIDER INTELLIGENCE. (1) ON 19TH NOVEMBER H.M.A.S. "SYDNEY" SANK ENEMY RAIDER IN POSITION 026° SOUTH 111° EAST. H.M.A.S. "SYDNEY" HAS NOT BEEN HEAD OF SINCE. LAST SEEN BURNING AMIDSHIPS AND AFT STEERING SOUTH AT 5 KNOTS. RAIDER WAS POSSIBLY RAIDER G NUMBER 41. 25 GERMAN NAVAL SURVIVORS PICKED BY "TROCAS" FROM RAFT 24/7(?). 2 RAIDERS LIFE BOATS LANDED NEAR CARNARVON WESTERN AUSTRALIA (?). STRICT CENSORSHIP IN FORCE AT PRESENT.

(11) AT 0550Z/23 H.M. F. S. "VITI" SIGHTED UNIDENTIFIED SUSPICIOUS VESSEL POSITION 010° SOUTH 177° WEST. DESCRIPTION 3 MASTS FLUSH DECK FUNNEL AFT APPARENTLY TANKER. COURSE 270.

(111) ON 22ND NOVEMBER H.M.S. "DEVONSHIRE" SANK ENEMY SHIP POSITION 004° SOUTH 018° WEST. MAY HAVE BEEN RAIDER C NUMBER 16.

stribution:
t N.M.
d N.M.
.C.N.S.
N.I.
N.B.
RECS.

Message sent 28 November 1941. Note position given, the censorship enforced, and that the *Sydney* was last seen steering south at five knots.

Sea Power Centre — Australia

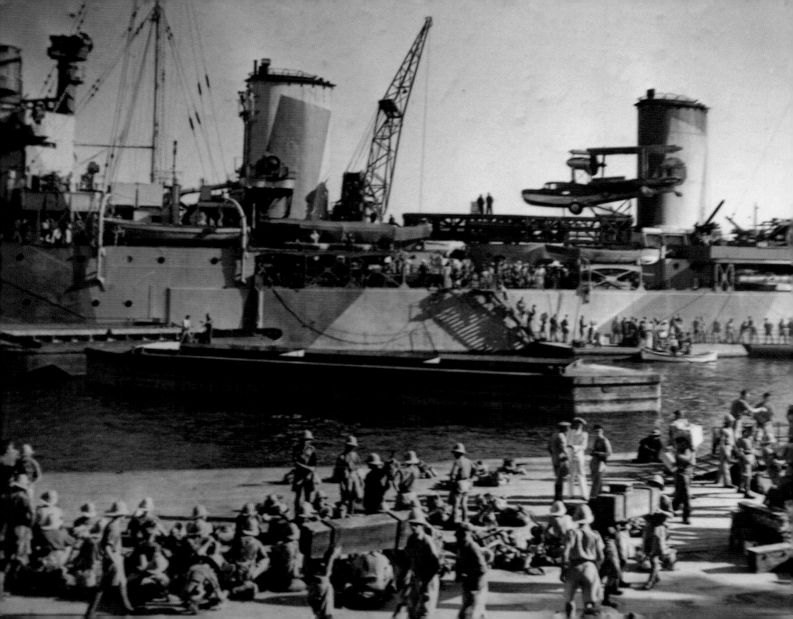

Left document (MESSAGE FORM):

Taken over phone ... 5 A.S.U.
by Signals Clerk South area Geraldton
... L/C Cooper

RAAF Form A.51
MESSAGE FORM

Call IN — 24·50/metres
and OUT — ... radio Geraldton under the
Preface

TO: ...

FROM: ... Mr Palmer (Batch)

R/T & morse | 2140 ... till 1125
" Calling during 0940 till 1125
" Calling Darwin or Technical Telegraph
operator — " Call from sea
Sydney calling send Corvel men
on board" — " Calling Frozit
D/F & Darwin — Cannot detect
you — " Singapore call Darwin —
This — H.S. Sydney calling
message received frequency
satisfactory will put it through in morse
(at 1110) Cpl Dawson & Readers ...
— Four stations transmitting on morse
on same wavelength —
" Sydney calling Darwin Distress — State

L/C Cooper

Right document:

2140 (Calling Darwin Telegraph Operator (Repeated
several times). Call from C.
Sydney calling. Send carved men
on board. all men on board
Calling Frozit D.M. Darwin
Cannot detect you. repeated
couple times.)

2150 "R.T. Sydney Calling Darwin
Distress signals Shunt
Leichardt. Send morse
after 2050. D S Z D."

2240 Singapore Call Darwin. A.S
Sydney calling 2150

2255 Message received Frequency
satisfactory will put through
in morse

Heard by ⎫   at Esplanade Hostel
3 women ⎬   on ordinary short wave
2 men   ⎭   Broadcast receiver
Cpl Dawson   phoned L/C Cooper at ...
                 L/C Cooper phoned area

... for telephone
... by phone from F/O Bogue
Geraldton 16 30 4/54

when he died in 1978. Sadly, his draft manuscript shows that he was prepared to fabricate evidence, rendering him the first of many in the modern era to do so.[13]

While one hoax surfaced during the war in the form of a message in a bottle, the next, and arguably the most sophisticated after Robotham, appeared in 1980 when a Dr W.P. Evans, a former army officer, advised that he had found a *Sydney* kitbag on the beach north of Kalbarri. It contained a wooden box, in which were authentic wartime memorabilia. There was also a 'letter of proceedings' (official diary), ostensibly typed by *Sydney*'s last surviving officer, a sub-lieutenant. It carried an account of *Kormoran* flying a false flag, the sighting of a Japanese submarine by *Sydney* and, among other things, *Kormoran* opening fire before surrendering. Then in the process of sending an anti-scuttling party boat across, *Sydney* was struck by a torpedo fired from *Kormoran*'s underwater tube.

It was all a fabrication: the bag, the box, its contents and the typescript were later proved by the Australian War Memorial (AWM) to be the result of an elaborate fraud. At the request of the Commonwealth Department of Home Affairs, which was then responsible historic wrecks, they established expert teams arguing for and against the evidence in the box.[14] Ultimately the department's scientists showed that the bag had been washed in fluorescing soap powder of a type not invented until the 1960s. The Western Australian Museum was also involved as part of its brief in managing reports of relics believed to be from historic vessels, and it advised that it was impossible for organic materials to survive the ravages of white ants in that environment. This staff had learnt while working the wreck and land camps associated with the Dutch East Indies Ship *Zuytdorp*, which lie along that same stretch of shore.[15]

Transcripts of signals once believed to have been from HMAS *Sydney* but found by the 2008 Commission of Inquiry to have 'come from the Post Master General in the city of Sydney'. (See Volume 3 of the COI Report '*Frauds, Conspiracies and Speculations*'.)

Australian National Archives

The wartime archives are opened

In 1975 the wartime archives were opened and Michael Montgomery, son of *Sydney* navigator Commander C.A.C. Montgomery, RN, came to Australia to examine them with a view to obtaining a satisfactory explanation for the loss of his father. In 1981 he published a provocative work entitled *Who Sank the* Sydney*?* adding further to the existing controversies raising awareness and concerns.[16] Other than those appearing above and a claim that the battle did not take place near the location given by T.A. Detmers these are, in the main, that *Kormoran* was lying in wait for the troopship *Aquitania*; that it had heaved to after receiving a salvo from *Sydney*, which injured part of the raider's crew; that *Sydney* had lowered a boat to render medical assistance, or to prevent scuttling; and that *Kormoran* had fired an underwater torpedo before hoisting its true colours. Finally, Montgomery claimed that there had been an official cover-up and that the lighthouse tender *Cape Otway* had subsequently found bodies and that its log was later tampered with, removing all relevant entries from the record. Also new to the burgeoning list of controversies at this time were claims that the *Kormoran* injured were deliberately abandoned rather than having been lost in a capsize of their life raft, as explained by Detmers in his interrogations and in his book on the voyage of the *Kormoran*.[17]

In April 1984 Barbara Poniewierski (writing as Barbara Winter), an Australian-born German-speaking scholar, and one of the experts who assisted in the examination of the Evans box, published *HMAS* Sydney*: Fact Fantasy and Fraud*. She too had been accessing the newly opened archives and very successfully challenged much of what appears in Michael Montgomery's work.[18] Rather than quashing speculation as

Geraldton-born Thomas Edgar Davis as a midshipman, 1937.

Western Australian Museum (donated by the Davis Family)

perhaps she had hoped, her attempts to counter Montgomery and other conspiracy theorists served to draw many otherwise passive observers into an increasingly acrimonious debate.

The press also became interested by the growing controversies, sadly willing to report even the most implausible and unsubstantiated stories relating to *Sydney*. These regularly appeared in the papers, as television news, as current affairs, and much later in the virtual media. In effect, by the mid-1990s no one really knew whom to believe and there was a pervading mistrust of government and of the German account in all but a few circles. As self-publishing became relatively easy, many books emerged carrying claims of German and Japanese atrocities, government conspiracy and cover-up. As the worldwide web developed, many conspiracy theorists developed email groups, which sometimes involved concerned relatives. Others developed websites carrying their theories and many produced quite startling claims. Some also claimed to have located *Sydney*. In one case there were claims to have located and identified both ships and a Japanese submarine using airborne technology (see following) and in another there were claims to have located the two ships using satellites. These received considerable interest — even from overseas navies — until in the latter case, the proponent also claimed to have found a Japanese aircraft carrier nearby. In these instances the 'inventors' hoped to promote and even sell their new 'technology'. Those calling for objectivity, including the Western Australian Museum, which had become responsible for the wrecks under the terms of the Commonwealth *Historic Shipwrecks Act 1976*, were regularly labelled as part of a whole-of-government cover-up.

PAGE 67

Able Seaman Rex Albert Cooper signing autographs for young boys on a tour of HMAS *Sydney*.

Glenys McDonald Collection (donated by the Cooper family)

"We as children always knew that there was something special about our father and we all miss him terribly — the hurt never went away …

"Our loss was unbelievable. Mother immediately tried to protect us from the immense grief and longing she felt. She explained the telegram to us. There was this thought that if father was 'lost at sea', then maybe he would turn up somewhere on an island in the Indian Ocean, or even be a prisoner of the Japanese … It could have been a terrible mistake and would all come right in the end."

BARBARA CRAILL
DAUGHTER OF ABLE SEAMAN WALTER EDWARD ALBERT FREER

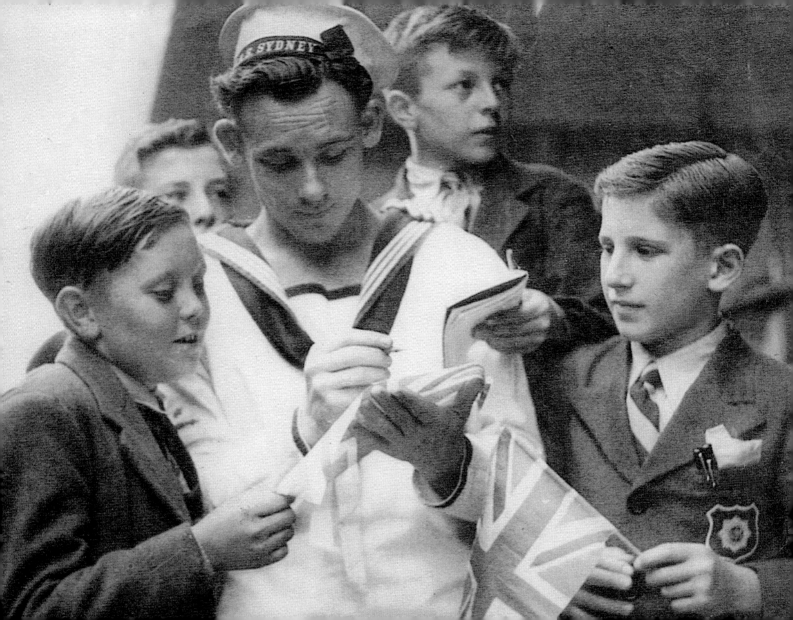

4

TOWARDS RESOLVING THE MYSTERIES

M. McCarthy

(Source: 'A précis of search-related events leading up to the commencement of the HMAS *Sydney* Search')[19]

The first searches for HMAS *Sydney*

Under the *Historic Shipwrecks Act 1976* (the Act) the minister responsible delegated to the director of the Western Australian Museum the task of managing historic wrecks off the coast of Western Australia. As a result staff were required to try and understand the *Sydney–Kormoran* mystery and they became responsible for the examination of reports that the wreck(s) had been found. The first examination of indications of a wreck believed to be related to HMAS *Sydney* occurred in 1981. It was based on Michael Montgomery's suggestion that *Sydney* might have headed in towards the coast before sinking and that indicators of the wreck might be found in coastal oil-search records.

This led to the finding of a very promising magnetic anomaly in (relatively) shallow waters off the Zuytdorp cliffs north of Kalbarri. As a result, Montgomery completed a standard report of finding a wreck or relic believed to be historic under the terms of the Act, and the way was thereby cleared for the expenditure of Commonwealth shipwreck funds in the inspection of the 'find'. As was standard practice whenever a wreck believed to be historic may have been found, the museum opened a specific-purpose wreck file (HMAS *Sydney* 630/81), entering in it all correspondence and notes on its research programs relative to both ships, the battle, and the search for the ship(s). At 56 volumes (not counting the new files opened after the wrecks were found), it is by far the largest of all the Western Australian Museum's files.

Being far too deep and too far offshore for the museum's workboats, the Royal Australian Navy (RAN) was requested to assist in the search, and in October 1981 a combined museum/RAN team joined on board the hydrographic survey ship HMAS *Moresby* to locate and analyse the anomaly. Using magnetometers, hull-mounted sonar, side-scan sonar, and the ship's echo sounder, the object was eventually proved to be a geological formation (probably a volcanic plug) lying c. 200 metres below the seabed.[20]

Thereafter, the museum and the RAN (to whom many also turned for answers), either independently or in harness, analysed, and in some cases examined, well over 25 *Sydney*-related reports. While some were fraudulent, or imaginary, many were promising echo-sounder traces that required official action. Some were based on reports of wreckage brought up in trawl nets and again these required official action under the Act. In this work the museum used funds provided by the Commonwealth's historic shipwrecks grant program for the required travel, accommodation, boat and equipment charters. A great deal of support was also provided gratis by oil industry vessels and by the armed services. All reports subsequently proved to be either unrelated wreckage or non-magnetic deepwater reefs, and if magnetic, were geological in origin.

The museum's 1991 Finding Sydney seminar

The location of SS *Titanic* and the German battleship *Bismarck* by the Woods Hole Oceanographic Institute (WHOI) in the mid 1980s posed the question: Could *Sydney* also be located? In July 1990 WHOI accepted an offer to join the museum in a non-disturbance search-and-survey program. In anticipation, permission was received from the many stakeholders, including the Commonwealth Government, the RAN, the Returned Services League, the German government and the Kormoran Survivors' Association. Further specialist support was provided in 1991 when local remote-sensing firms (ASI, Aerodata, Fugro McLelland) offered their services in the search.[21]

> " *L. Knight [and W. Whittaker] — claims to have located three vessels off Abrolhos Islands using his Subtle Energy Detection System — ships identified as HMAS Sydney, HSK Kormoran and an unknown Japanese.* "
>
> Western Australian Museum HMAS *Sydney* file note [22]

Then the museum, together with the shipwrecks unit at the Commonwealth Department of Home Affairs, developed contingency plans for the protection of the wrecks, should they be found. This included the declaring of a restricted zone around the site(s) prohibiting access for all bar bona fide research purposes. In the face of ongoing claims that important materials were missing, and in order to be best place to provide advice, the museum also embarked on fact-finding searches of archives in Canberra, Perth, Melbourne and elsewhere, again using historic shipwrecks program funds.

Following a suggestion from cognitive scientist Dr Kim Kirsner of the University of Western Australia, who was also researching *Sydney*, the museum convened a commemorative seminar and the opening of an exhibit on the *Sydney* on the 50th anniversary of its loss. Researchers; serving and retired naval personnel; archivists; oceanographers; climatologists; search-and-rescue operatives, e.g. the Australian Maritime Safety Authority (AMSA); the Bureau of Meteorology; the Royal

Australian Navy Hydrographic Service and other experts gathered at the museum on 19 November 1991 for the forum. Proceedings were opened by Commodore Peter Briggs AM, Naval Officer Commanding Western Australia. Letters of support were read from Otto Jürgensen, representing the Kormoran Survivors' Association, and the Honourable Kim Beazley, then a leading minister in the Commonwealth Government. These, and the many papers and discussions that followed, were recorded and collated for the major archives and institutions.[23]

With a view to a possible search, one of the key questions put to the oceanographers, climatologists and search-and-rescue specialists present was the issue of whether the spread of wreckage (not counting anything that could have been propelled or steered) supported Detmers' assertion that the battle took place near 26°34'S 111°E, c. 120 nautical miles south-west of Shark Bay.[24] The answer was unequivocally 'yes'. On the other hand, the notion that *Sydney* could be found was dealt a severe blow when the specialists were unable to reduce the search area down to anything like the proportions of the two previously successful deepwater searches, i.e. around 500 square kilometres. In contrast the area in which *Sydney* was thought to lie was a vast c. 7200 square kilometres, far too large an area for the equipment available at that time.[25] It was with all those imponderables in mind that WHOI understandably declined to proceed with the search.

Many researchers, too numerous to list, provided their assistance and insights to the museum as it pursued the eight recomendations of the 1991 forum, including the need to commence the search with the archives. Some came to produce work of such quality and import that their research was published or accepted for

John and Mollie Ross on their honeymoon, Sydney, December 1941. John Ross was transferred out of HMAS *Sydney*, and before taking his new post at HMAS *Canberra* was granted permission to marry.

Western Australian Museum (W.H. [John] Ross Collection)

Sydney crew members after the
Battle of Cape Spada, 1940.
Photograph taken by Able Seaman
Anthony Arthur Bodman. A
photograph of him appears on page
52.

RSL, Geraldton

listing under the museum's report series. One was an analysis of the possible and probable search areas for *Sydney* produced by Kim Kirsner and Sam Hughes of AMSA.[26] Others were by Wes Olson, an independent researcher who not only proved that the Carley float recovered at Christmas Island was from *Sydney*, but also showed where it had come from on the ship. He also produced a comparative study examining other ships, losses and engagements where similar damage to that inflicted on *Sydney* also resulted.[27] Later these reports evolved into an exhaustively researched and highly acclaimed book.[28] Some of the researchers who provided exceptional service to the museum were later granted honorary associate status — a rare honour.[29] On the other hand, in this same period some other researchers, while sometimes providing otherwise very useful and important insights, also came to espouse conspiracy theory. Though advised to remain objective and provide references or corroborative evidence for the claims being made, they invariably failed to do so and, sadly, continued to produce unsubstantiated and, from the museum's perspective, unpublishable speculation. Their findings were filed or entered into the archive nonetheless.

A few years after the 1991 forum some researchers turned their attention to the area off Port Gregory and the nearby Abrolhos Islands as a possible location for *Sydney* as it tried to make the coast.[30] Though opinion on this possibility was divided,[31] some took it a step further and concluded that the battle had taken place in that region and that Detmers' battle position off Shark Bay was false. This notion received added impetus with the location of two (relatively) shallow-water magnetic anomalies in the area north of the Abrolhos Islands. This became front-page news, with headlines and

In many hearts, the SYDNEY still lives

The 50th anniversary of the SYDNEY's disappearance saw a host of activities planned.

The Western Australian Maritime Museum was to host its HMAS SYDNEY Forum from 19 to 21 November, including a SYDNEY display, a memorial service at the Kings Park War Memorial and two days of presentations and discussions on the subject.

There were two purposes — to focus firstly on the proposed search for the SYDNEY and the KORMORAN and secondly, on continuing management issues such as site management and war graves status should either vessel be found as well as conservation, restoration and display of artefacts.

The WA Maritime Museum was gathering together a team consisting of the RAN, the Woods Hole Oceanographic Institute (finders of TITANIC and BISMARK), the Australian Remote Sensing firm Associated Survey International, the Centre for Marine Science and Technology at Curtin University, and the WA Maritime Museum itself, to begin the process of instigating a search for the SYDNEY.

The team was being assisted by the RAN, the Australian War Memorial, CSIRO, the Australian Maritime Safety Authority, the Bureau of Meteorology, Steedman Science and Engineering, and by many associations, museums, authors and historians.

Carnarvon was to be a focal point for remembrance of the SYDNEY.

Participants at ceremonies on Saturday 23 November were to include the patrol boat HMAS DUBBO, senior RAN personnel, five RAAF Macchi jet trainers from RAAF Pearce, Federal and State parliamentarians, local civic leaders and schoolchildren.

The most poignant moment of remembrance was bound to be the Kings Park service on 19 November when the surviving members of the SYDNEY Association, former crew members of the cruiser, gathered for one last tribute under their own banner.

Their numbers had dwindled to the point that, from 1992, they were to join the Naval Association and pay homage on 4 October to the loss of all RAN ships and the men who served in them.

At Carnarvon, alongside the town's war memorial, a brick Wall of Remembrance bearing the names of all the men who died with the SYDNEY was to be unveiled.

At High Rock, on Quobba sheep station at 5.30pm on the same day, a simple ceremony was to be held at a monument built to honour a wonderful ship and 645 men who paid the supreme sacrifice.

This unusual view of SYDNEY harks back to her arrival in Fremantle in 1936. Her bow paintwork battered by a long and rough Indian Ocean crossing, she is low on fuel and thus rides high in the water.

A report of Western Australian activities for the 50th anniversary of the disappearance of HMAS *Sydney*, 1991.

V. Miller and M. McCarthy (WAM) for No Survivors, WA Newspapers.

newsagents banners stating that *Sydney* had been found. There was also considerable interest in a number of other anomalies in the same region. Subsequent analysis by the RAN and remote-sensing specialists Aerodata, who provided their services gratis, proved them all to be geological in origin. Nevertheless, the extensive publicity swung public attention to these claims and to the possibility that either or both wrecks lay in the Abrolhos area. This interest was reinforced when experienced navigators, including some past and serving RAN officers, concluded that the lifeboats that landed north of Carnarvon must have emanated from the Abrolhos region and not from the Detmers' battle position west of Shark Bay. Added to this, and, surprisingly, receiving considerable press, were claims that *Sydney*, *Kormoran* and an unidentified Japanese vessel (later claimed to be a submarine) had been found, as indicated in the previous chapter. This 'find' was achieved using a combination of 'map dowsing'[32] and the controversial Subtle Energy Detection System, later called the Knight Direct Location System (KDLS) after its inventor. In essence this system comprised a small black box

> " … [the] first step in any 'in-water' search for HMAS Sydney *would be to examine an area at or near 26°32–34'S 111°E.*"
>
> Western Australian Museum Parliamentary Inquiry submission[33]

that the inventor claimed was capable of locating and also identifying deepwater wrecks and their contents while being carried in a light aircraft. While scientists were entirely skeptical, many researchers and even some of the bereaved families came to defend the system fiercely, roundly criticising any, including the Western Australian Museum, who denied its validity. This all proved to have disastrous consequences, delaying the search by well over a decade (see page 86).

As a result of the escalating publicity, a forum was held in 1996 in Geraldton and another in Fremantle in February 1997. These were followed by a parliamentary inquiry by the Joint Standing Committee on Foreign Affairs, Defence and Trade and an exhaustive round of hearings that was held across Australia in 1997–98 with a view to accounting for the loss of *Sydney* and developing a way forward in resolving the mystery. Its six-part brief included examining the extent to which all available archival materials had been evaluated, reporting on the practicality of locating and identifying the grave on Christmas Island, and advising on the best means of protecting the sites if and when found. After collating all the evidence received by voluntary submissions into an 18-volume set, the committee produced its report in 1999, making 17 recommendations. One included a search of the British archives, and two others read:

Recommendation 10: *The Royal Australian Navy sponsor a seminar on the likely search areas for Sydney and Kormoran, involving as many of the individual researchers and groups as possible.*

Recommendation 11: *After the search area is more accurately defined, some preliminary surveys be undertaken to try and confirm the accuracy of the wreck locations, prior to a full in-water search. An initial search for HSK Kormoran at or near 26°32–34'S, 111°E, if supported by the seminar, would seem a logical starting point.*[34]

As a result, naval historian, author and former head of Defence Studies, Captain

Peter Hore, RN (Retd) was commissioned with a search of the British Archives.[35] An official HMAS *Sydney* Wreck Location Seminar was also convened. Hosted by the RAN's Sea Power Centre, it was held at the Western Australian Maritime Museum in November 2001 as a 60th anniversary of the sinking event.[36] Though designed to more accurately define the potential search area for the wrecks, organisers found the attendees implacably split between proponents of a northern (Detmers' area) and a southern (Abrolhos area) battle position.[37] The museum's attempts to broker a behind-the-scenes compromise agreement that would see Detmers' position in the northern area searched first, and if unsuccessful, then the southern sites, failed dismally. This all led the chair to conclude that

> *… more research … is needed so that those who have to make the decisions about using large amounts of money, at least some of it public money, can do so on the best possible and informed basis. I have to say as a concluding comment, that I am disappointed that several years on from the parliamentary report and given all the work various groups here today have been doing, a greater measure of agreement and precision does not yet seem to be emerging. Until it does, talk of mounting searches at this stage is still premature.*[38]

When its own plans for a search and any hope of receiving funding evaporated due to withdrawal of Woods Hole in the mid 1990s, the museum assumed a support role, providing advice and assistance to researchers, and to a series of trusts and foundations subsequently formed to fill the vacuum. The first was the HMAS Sydney Trust, led by Wayne Sydney Born. It was formed in 1995 with the backing of a number of politicians, including the Honourable Graham

Bombs drop from enemy aircraft off the stern of HMAS *Sydney* after she sank the *Bartolomeo Colleoni*, Mediterranean, 19 July 1940.

Australian War Memorial Negative Number 306693

Edwards, a parliamentarian and former serviceman who had been severely injured and had lost both his legs in battle. Sadly, the trust folded soon after Born died, apparently as result of the privations suffered during their first attempt to examine a seabed anomaly off Carnarvon.[39] It was followed by the HMAS Sydney Foundation, led by Ed Punchard, then a recent graduate of the museum's course in maritime archaeology. He was also a budding filmmaker whose first projects included an international award-winning film on *Sydney* entitled *No Survivors*.[40] Under Punchard, the foundation garnered wider national political support and was also instrumental in effecting the 1997–98 parliamentary inquiry.[41] When the foundation folded, it was followed in 2001 by HMAS Sydney Search Pty Ltd, led by former leading members of the earlier foundation Ted Graham, a principal of a local remote-sensing firm, and Dr Kim Kirsner, together with Dr Don Pridmore, a remote-sensing specialist who had also been very active in earlier promoting a search for *Sydney*. Later they were joined by Ron Birmingham QC, Bob King (OAM), Commodore Bob Trotter, RAN (Retd), as CEO, and finally Keith Rowe and Glenys McDonald (AM). Under Graham's leadership, this group built on their predecessor's success in developing an increasingly higher profile; high-powered political, naval and academic support; and greater public credibility.[42] Like the museum before them, all these groups considered the Detmers' position of 26°34'S 111°E the focal point for any search.

Around 2002, convinced he could find the wrecks despite the 2001 Wreck Location Seminar findings, highly successful deepwater searcher David Mearns of Sussex-based Blue Water Recoveries — finder of HMS *Hood* and numerous other deepwater sites — began making contact with the RAN, the museum and HMAS Sydney Search Pty Ltd. As a proven deepwater wreck finder, along with WHOI, the museum strongly supported Mearns' candidacy as a service provider to the RAN and to HMAS Sydney Search Pty Ltd.

In his letter to then chief of naval staff, David Mearns advised that in his preliminary reading he was particularly struck by the findings of the 2001 Sea Power Centre seminar's archival committee, led by Wes Olson. This committee, of which Captain Peter Hore was a member, had concluded that the Detmers' position (26°34'S 111°E) was *Kormoran's* noontime location, and from their calculations the battle itself took place within a few nautical miles of 26°S 111°E.[43] They also concluded that there was a 'reasonable chance' that the wreck of HMAS *Sydney* was lying within 15 nautical miles of the *Kormoran* towards the south-east. While they believed that oil sighted by aircraft during the war five nautical miles south-east of 26°S 111°E was possibly from the wreck, the committee also acknowledged that if *Sydney* had stayed afloat longer than the German statements suggested, it could lie up to 100 nautical miles to the south-south-east of that position.[44] This consideration, and the fact that during the war the RAN thought there was a possibility *Sydney* may have recovered enough to try and make for the nearest naval base in Sourabaya or Singapore, remained nagging doubts for any intending searchers.

According to Ted Graham, chair of the HMAS Sydney Search Pty Ltd, which also became known as the Finding Sydney Foundation (FSF), both it and its predecessor used Kim Kirsner and his associate Dr John Dunn's research to narrow down the FSF search box. In later explaining this process, Professor Kirsner advised that, with

HMAS *Sydney* boat badge.

Sea Power Centre — Australia

NAVAL MESSAGE

WD GA   **NAVY OFFICE.**

COPY OF MESSAGE.

To.............ADMIRALTY, C. IN C. CHINA, C. IN C. EAST INDIES, C.Z.M.,
N.Z.N.B., FO.C.A.S.

From.........A.C.N.B.

Method of Transmission.............W.T.   { P/L. CODE. CONF. CODE. CYP.   A.F. CYPHER

Date and Time Sent.............29/11/41

Date and Time Received.............

Originator's Number.............Time of Origin.............1254Z/29

ORTANT.   S E C R E T

N.B.'S 0249Z/29

THE N.B. REGRET THAT AFTER INTENSIVE AIR AND SURFACE SEARCH
OF THE AREA NO EVIDENCE OF H.M.A.S."SYDNEY" HAS BEEN SIGHTED
EXCEPT TWO R.A.N. LIFE BELTS AND ONE CARLEY FLOAT BADLY
DAMAGED BY GUNFIRE. IT IS CONCLUDED THAT "SYDNEY" SANK
AFTER THE ACTION AND FURTHER SEARCH HAS BEEN ABANDONED.

(ABOVE WILL ALSO HAVE TO BE PASSED TO 'CANBERRA FOR THE
G.G., P.M. & MINISTER FOR NAVY ALSO MR SHEDDO N. ALSO
PASS TO N.O.I.C.DARWIN FOR 1stN.M.)

the assistance of the Australian War Memorial, the Australian Research Council and the University of Western Australia, he and Dr Dunn used their expertise in cognitive science to verify the German accounts and to produce a 400-square-nautical-mile search rectangle centred close to 26°S 111°E.[45] In joining with Captain Hore, David Mearns had also come to the conclusion that the German account was reliable, and he believed that these findings were sufficient to see the RAN reverse its earlier decision not to support a search.[46] In 2004 the FSF opened negotiations with Mearns and a number of meetings were held, resulting in their signing of a Memorandum of Understanding by year's end. Though Kim Kirsner left the FSF in late November 2004,[47] the foundation continued to use the Kirsner–Dunn research, considering it and the Mearns–Hore findings as 'pivotal' in 'determining the search box'. The FSF then presented what Chairman Ted Graham characterised as 'the confluence' of all this research in submissions to government, corporate and private sponsors from 2005 through to 2007, when the search was announced.[48]

In 2005, satisfied that there was enough agreement on the need to search the Detmers' position, the Honourable John Howard, the then prime minister, announced a grant of $1.3 million dollars to HMAS Sydney Search Pty Ltd to pursue the search. It then established a Memorandum of Understanding, with Mearns as its chosen in-water operative. The Western Australian Government also provided support to enable the company to function.

Despite the agreement of all of the above as to the appropriate search location, proponents of a southern battle position near the Abrolhos Islands remained vociferous in pointing to numerous unresolved reports of possible sites in that region. Local and overseas oil-search companies brought together by John Begg of Voyager Energy then approached the museum offering their expertise.[49] They subsequently combined to examine gratis (and at quite considerable expense to themselves) eight 'Sydney'-related' sites that had been reported in that area, all showing to be either geological or non-existent. This left only the very deepwater sites supposedly located by the mysterious KDLS system.

Despite the method having been unequivocally dismissed as scientifically impossible in the lead-up to the 2001 SPC seminar, the evidence which would have entirely destroyed any support for the KDLS method was not tabled there.[50] As a result there remained a number of vocal adherents who continued to view the failure to search the KDLS positions as evidence of a government 'cover-up'. The museum, especially, was criticised for failing to give the KDLS system any credence at all and for having made public its denial that the KDLS sites were *Sydney*, *Kormoran* or a Japanese submarine, as claimed in 2002 in the local press.

In March 2007, and on behalf of the FSF, Perth-based Geo Subsea Pty Ltd, which had its research vessel MV *Geosounder* travelling en route Fremantle to Dampier, investigated gratis one of the KDLS sites off the Abrolhos Islands. Using a state-of-the-art, multi-beam, echo-sounder system capable of mapping the seabed for a distance of three kilometres either side to a depth of 5000 metres, nothing but a bare seabed was found. This served to remove unequivocally the KDLS positions from the agenda. Together with the 2002 'Begg' findings, these results also rendered beyond doubt the 'southern sites' of secondary, if any, importance in any search-and-survey regime. The way was finally opened for government to

A facsimile of the original billboard produced for the 50th anniversary commemorations.

Western Australian Museum

provide full financial support to the search of Detmers' position at or around, plus or minus a degree (i.e. 60 nautical miles), 26°34'S 111°E.

Even then it was all nearly derailed again when in August 2007 front-page news and national TV prime-time slots were filled with images provided by a team that thought they had found *Sydney* in relatively shallow water off Shark Bay. This occurred despite the museum earlier advising Shark Bay interests that a bolt they had earlier recovered from the site (and whose details they had tried to suppress for many years) could not have been from either *Sydney* or its adversary *Kormoran*.

Unable to effect its own inspection due to the water depth, again the museum sought RAN assistance, resulting in an examination of the area by the survey ship HMAS *Leeuwin*. This showed that the site was that of a small wooden-hulled vessel, most likely a trawler — as earlier advised by the museum — and clearly not related to *Sydney* or its adversary. After a short delay and often-heated public debate, caused by the need to attend to this claim, the Honourable Bruce Billson, the then minister assisting the minister for defence, announced a total Commonwealth grant of $4.2 million for the search. This, when joined with the $500,000 provided by the Western Australian Government, a further $250,000 from the New South Wales Government, and some public and corporate sponsorship, made a search for *Sydney* and, as a necessary preliminary, *Kormoran* finally possible. Subsequently, at a ceremony held at the Maritime Museum on 19 November 2007, HMAS Sydney Search Pty Ltd formally launched what was to ultimately be a successful search. One of the speeches delivered on that occasion was why the search for *Sydney* had taken so long.[51]

PAGE 89

Members of the crew of HMAS *Sydney* in front of one of the ship's gun mounts: Able Seaman Douglas James Burrowes (back row, right); 22831 Able Seaman Robert Underdown Ewens (front row, left); and two unidentified sailors.

Australian War Memorial Negative Number PO6804.002

"At the time we received the telegram I was eight years old, and will never forget those few weeks … Mr and Mrs Dyer, the local postmaster and his wife had waited till the post office closed for the day and had walked the long distance to personally deliver the telegram. My mother screamed and we all cried, not realising just what was wrong. Then came the worst years of our lives. Our mother did not cope with the uncertainty; she walked the floor night after night … I waited till the end of the war always expecting my dad to return."

MARGARET MORSE
DAUGHTER OF PETTY OFFICER COOK JOHN STANLEY DAVEY

5

THE SUCCESSFUL SEARCH

M. McCarthy

(Sources: David Mearns, *The Search for the* Sydney; HMAS Sydney Search Pty. Ltd., Final report: The search
to find and identify the wrecks of HMAS *Sydney* II and HSK *Kormoran*; D.J. Perryman, Report on the search
for the wrecks of HMAS *Sydney* & HSK *Kormoran*, February–April 2008; M. McCarthy, the HMAS *Sydney*/
HSK *Kormoran* Wreck Inspection Daybook)[52]

Concluding the research

In 1991 the Museum's HMAS *Sydney* seminar concluded that to find the wreck of HMAS *Sydney*, HSK *Kormoran*, which lay in the vicinity of the Detmers' position of 26°34'S 111°E, would have to be found first. With the evidence about *Sydney*'s movements after the battle still remaining inconclusive, search leader David Mearns indicated that a 'dense cloud of uncertainty' still remained in his mind about when and where *Sydney* sank. As a result he elected to ignore all prior research, including the Kirsner and Dunn findings for the FSF, and go back to first principles. In his report and in his 2009 book, Mearns advised why he did so.[53] He also outlined the process whereby he started from scratch, and the support provided by Captain Hore and Wes Olson.

By this process Mearns came to have even more reason to believe Detmers' account of the battle and the position he had given. He had found new material at the Naval Historical Branch at Great Scotland Yard that had apparently lain unnoticed since 1947. Though providing different positions for the engagement, including another diagram showing the course of the battle, it again corroborated Detmers' account. When he found yet another *Gefechtsbericht* (action report) by Detmers, it became increasingly evident to Mearns and his team that Detmers had taken extraordinary measures to create and maintain this action report. One of these was transmitted back to Germany via Dr Habben, *Kormoran*'s medical officer, who memorised it and presented it as a verbal report when he was repatriated in 1943 as part of a prisoner exchange. It was subsequently published in December 1943 as a German naval staff battle summary, copies of which were captured by the British at the end

The forward funnel, torn from the *Sydney* in the descent to the seabed (see page 27).

Australian War Memorial (David Mearns/ Finding Sydney Foundation)

of the war. Five different reports or accounts, all emanating from Detmers and all supporting the location he gave, were eventually assessed by Hore and Mearns. The first had been created in early 1942 and was cleverly hidden as barely discernible dots under letters appearing in a German–English dictionary that had been given to Detmers while a prisoner. As a result of advice from Olson and Barbara Poniewierski (Winter) who had tabled it at the museum's HMAS *Sydney* Forum in 1991, Mearns and Hore eventually found it in Detmers' nephew's possession. As a primary source, a complete work, the original account — the sort of thing all wreck searchers dream of finding — was definitive.[54]

Despite becoming convinced of Detmers' veracity, and despite the research produced earlier, including that of Olson's 2001 archival committee, the problem still remained in Mearns' mind whether the Detmers' position was the noon position of *Kormoran* — the place where the two ships met in the evening, the start of the battle — or the sinking position. To that end a great deal of additional research was conducted and this was

> *" Theodor Detmers … had deceived his guards by hiding his battle report in the pages."*
>
> Peter Hore[55]

followed by further scientific analyses of the wind, surface current conditions and other variables by specialists, including a team from CSIRO and the Australian Bureau of Meteorology.[56] Funded by the FSF, these analyses showed Mearns that, while it was certainly possible that the German liferafts found at sea could have been launched from 26°34'S 111°E, it was 'far more probable' that they left the ship c. 30' further north. This placed *Kormoran* at around 26°S 111°E.

The search phase

David Mearns advises in the FSF report and in his subsequent book that after he had completed his research and received the advice of his scientists, he developed a search box that was to be examined using side-scan sonar. Having won the contract to provide this equipment and their expertise to the FSF, Seattle-based Williamson & Associates Inc sent out two deepwater 'sonar towfish' (SM-30 and AMS-60) units and their expert staff under the leadership of Art Wright. They were to board the MV *Geosounder*, the vessel contracted to the FSF and owned by Western Australian-based DOF Subsea Australia Pty Ltd, which had also won a contract for the job. This vessel came with precision navigation equipment and a dynamic positioning system (DPS) that allowed it to maintain station in all bar the roughest seas, expert navigators, and, should the wreck(s) be found, a remotely operated vehicle (ROV) rated to a maximum depth of 3000 metres, again with specialist operators.

In the FSF report on this phase Mearns advises that the survey of what was originally intended to be a 69-kilometre by 108-kilometre search area was conducted between 29 February and 20 March 2008. Twelve parallel, north/south-oriented 'primary lines' were planned by him, each having a sonar swathe width of 6000 metres, with each line around 110 kilometres in length and a run-line spacing of c. 3500 metres to ensure 100 percent sonar coverage. With the side-scan sonar 'fish' streamed out on a cable sometimes up to 9,000 metres behind the survey ship in order to maintain a height of around 350 metres above the seabed, *Geosounder* needed to travel at around two to three knots.

Williamson & Associates' side-scan sonar being deployed.

Finding Sydney Foundation

Side-scan sonar image of
HMAS *Sydney*.

Williamson & Associates/Finding Sydney
Foundation

The side-scan sonar survey, which was dogged by bad weather (Cyclone Ophelia), problems with the ship and gear failures, was initially concentrated around the central and eastern portion of the box. Four of the twelve run-lines were completed (lines six to nine) using the low-resolution SM-30 unit before the *Kormoran* wreck site was located in 2560 metres of water just a few nautical miles south of 26°S 111°E at 1730 hrs on 12 March 2008.[57] Then a high-resolution survey line using the AMS-60 unit was run in order to investigate what was thought to be the possible battle site. This was later shown to be an area with large boulders on the seabed and not the battle position. Having eliminated this position and using *Kormoran* as the datum, the search for HMAS *Sydney* was 'further refined' and two of the original 12 north/south run-lines (lines 11 and 12) were then surveyed across a 37-kilometre by 37-kilometre *Sydney* survey area using the SM-30 sonar again on a 6-kilometre swath setting.[58] By this means the *Sydney* wreck site was located in around 2460 metres of water only a few nautical miles away from *Kormoran* towards the south-east at 1103 hrs on 16 March 2008.[59] Three high-resolution survey lines were subsequently run at swathe widths of three kilometres, 1.5 kilometres and 750 metres to further investigate the site. Finally the AMS-60 system was deployed on a swathe width of 600 metes for a high-resolution pass parallel to the hull sections of each ship.

With David Mearns and his navigators fixing *Kormoran* at 26°05'46"S 111°04'33"E and then *Sydney* around 12 nautical miles away to the south east at 26°14'31"S 111°12'48"E, the positions posited by Mearns and Hore, and by Olson and his 2001 SPC committee using historical data; and by Kirsner and Dunn using cognitive science, have all proved remarkably accurate.[60] For those

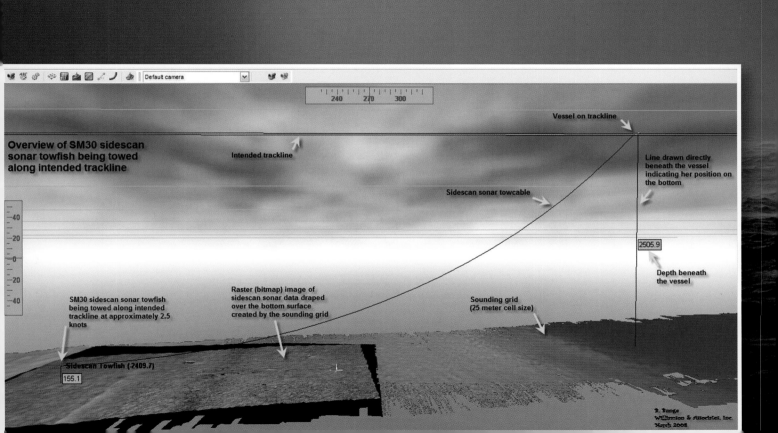

Overview of SM30 sidescan sonar towfish being towed along intended trackline

Intended trackline

Vessel on trackline

Sidescan sonar towcable

Line drawn directly beneath the vessel indicating her position on the bottom

2505.9

Depth beneath the vessel

SM30 sidescan sonar towfish being towed along intended trackline at approximately 2.5 knots

Raster (bitmap) image of sidescan sonar data draped over the bottom surface created by the sounding grid

Sounding grid (25 meter cell size)

Sidescan Towfish (-2409.7)

155.1

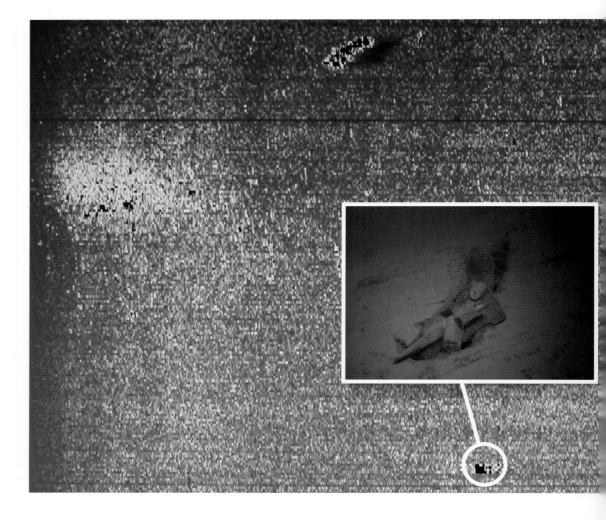

Side-scan sonar image of the HSK *Kormoran* wreck site. Showing (top) the bow section, (left) the debris field and (bottom right, circled) the engine room.

Williamson and Associates/Finding Sydney Foundation

INSERT: HSK *Kormoran* starboard anchor embedded in the engine room plating (see page 108).

Australian War Memorial (David Mearns/ Finding Sydney Foundation)

"At 00.35 there was a tremendous explosion and the whole stern and midships of the vessel turned into one gigantic sheet of flame which shot into the air perhaps a thousand feet high. And a little after that a shower of small debris fell all around us. Even at that time we were only about a thousand feet away, but fortunately we again came to no harm. When the vast flame had died down the *Kormoran* lifted her bows into the air and slipped backwards under the surface."

T.A. DETMERS[61]

unaware, a minute of latitude is one nautical mile. All involved had good cause to be very satisfied with their results. Of future scientific importance, it is evident that cognitive science can prove useful and that it could be factored in as a potential tool in any shipwreck or survivor-search regime. With the benefit of hindsight it is also evident that the two World War II naval signals mentioned earlier, one expressing the belief that the German raider had sunk at 26°S 111°E and the other in which it was 'assumed' that *Sydney* had sunk at 26°31'S 111°E were also remarkably accurate.

The ROV phase

Using funds provided by the Department of the Environment, Water, Heritage and the Arts (DEWHA), who administer the *Historic Shipwrecks Act 1976* and Historic Shipwrecks Program, the editor was requested to join the ship on its return to Geraldton as official observer for DEWHA in the examination of each wreck. Already onboard as observers during the search phase were Glenys McDonald (AM), acting for the FSF; and Lieutenant D.J. Perryman (RANR), senior naval historical officer, representing the RAN and the SPC.

As soon as *Geosounder* docked at the Geraldton wharf, all bar two of the Williamson crew and their gear were replaced by the operators of the Comanche sub-Atlantic ROV, their support crew and gear. With *Geosounder* maintaining steady position via satellite and its DPS system, the ROV, inside a protective cage or 'garage', was to be winched on a very strong cable containing its electrical wiring down to a position just above the wrecks. In the depths in which the ships were found, this was expected

LEFT: Remotely operated vehicle in its TMS (garage) waiting to be lowered to the seabed.

John Perryman

BELOW: ROV operator at the controls on board MV *Geosounder*. Top right on his console is the ROV leaving its 'garage'.

Western Australian Museum (M. McCarthy)

to take around one hour from surface to seabed. Then the ROV was to be piloted out by the operators, who were housed in a converted shipping container welded to the *Geosounder's* deck. It would then examine the wrecks and on completion would re-enter its garage for the slow trip back to the surface.

In the ROV phase, strict non-disturbance parameters were set by DEWHA as a condition of entry into the restricted zones that had been declared as soon as each site had been found. These agreements limited the ROV to the outside of each wreck, prohibited it approaching closer than two metres to any object, and strictly prohibited the recovery of any object. The umbilical linking the ROV to its garage was also required to remain clear of any wreckage, and even the seabed was protected from the ROV's propeller wash by the requirement to remain well above it.

The Electric Pictures' German-born cameraman, Ullrick Krafzik, who had been troubled by the *Kormoran* disguising itself to deceive the Allies until informed that *Sydney* had previously used a similar ruse.

Western Australian Museum (M. McCarthy)

Mechanical and electrical problems encountered during preparation and testing alongside the wharf, together with the very heavy weather (Cyclone Pancho) in the search area, delayed ROV operations until 29 March. Then there were to be sea trials and a long traverse from port out to the site(s) before more trials on site. Yet again there were problems with the ROV. Though fully operational in all its rigorous surface checks, at one stage it refused to 'fly' out of its protective garage while being held in position only a few tantalising metres away from the wreck of *Sydney*, which was visible in the background. Rather than raise it up with no result, the first record of *Sydney* was produced by moving *Geosounder* slowly around the wreck, with the 'garage' dangling over 2000 metres below and the ROV firmly stuck inside. This all attested to the skill of the ship's captain and the specialist seabed navigator, aided by *Geosounder's* dynamic position-keeping systems.[62] After then

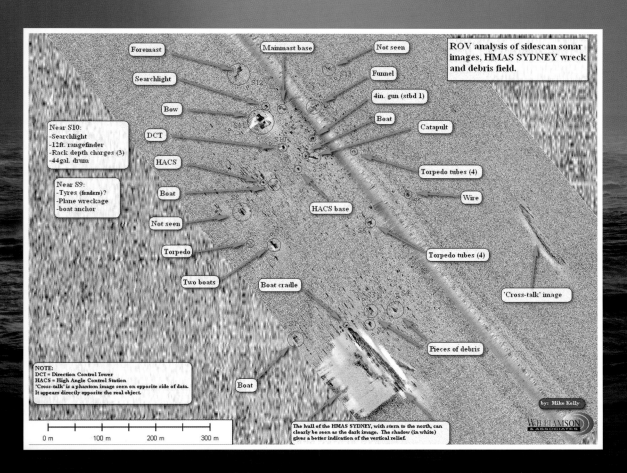

The ROV was sent to examine each of the large pieces of wreckage near the *Sydney* hull. Once identified Mike Kelly of Williamson & Associates entered them onto this site plan.

A close-up of the propellors on the seabed.

Australian War Memorial (David Mearns/ Finding Sydney Foundation)

INSET: The stern and port propellor of HMAS *Sydney* (II) at the ship's launch, 1934.

Western Australian Museum (H.J. Watson Collection).

being beset by some very rough seas, it all eventually came together. The ROV and its cameras performed admirably and the survey proper began, continuing through to 9 April 2008.

While the ROV operators were on deck, David Mearns, the observers and the specialists were all in a compartment deep in the bowels of *Geosounder*, giving directions, tracing paths along and across each ship, conferring, photographing and recording in still and video form from every possible angle. Aided by Lieutenant Perryman, who had earlier completed a detailed study of the ship and who had obtained detailed builder's plans, Mearns proceeded to target and identify features on *Sydney*. Armed also with plans he had obtained from Germany of *Kormoran*, Mearns then directed a similar regime for what remained of the German ship. Logs were kept of the movement of the ROV, and each observer maintained a record of events and provided advice where appropriate.

Unexpectedly, for it had been anticipated from previous experience at other shipwrecks that each ship would lie partly buried in sediment, both wrecks were found with their lower hulls almost totally exposed down to the bilge keels. This allowed their lower hulls to be examined for torpedo damage, a most unexpected boon for the inspection team. When added to the evidence of damage above the waterline, this was to prove essential to those analysing the data in what was to be the next phase in resolving the mysteries surrounding the loss of *Sydney*.

PAGE 113

The lord mayor of Perth, Sir Thomas Meagher, with members of the HMAS *Sydney* crew, February 1941.

West Australian Newspapers

from the HMAS *Sydney* (II) site. LEFT: one of *Sydney*'s 4-inch Quick Firing Mark V anti-aircraft guns in situ on her wreck. TOP LEFT: *Sydney*'s b[...] just above the sea bed. TOP RIGHT: the damaged gun housing of *Sydney*'s B turret. BOTTOM LEFT: one of a number of leather shoes found l[...] *Sydney*'s debris field. BOTTOM RIGHT: one of *Sydney*'s cutters with her distinctive badge still visible on the bow (see page 83).

...rom the HSK *Kormoran* site. TOP LEFT: the No. 3 5.9-inch gun, with blistered paint due to high rate of firing. TOP RIGHT: the shank of *Kor*...ed starboard anchor. The flukes severed from it during the ships destruction (see page 98). BOTTOM LEFT: the open concealment flap of *Korm*...board above water torpedo tubes. BOTTOM RIGHT: an underwater torpedo tube opening. RIGHT: the port anchor still secure in its hawse pi...

EXTRACT FROM THE WRECK INSPECTOR'S DAYBOOK

M. McCarthy, Western Australian Museum

Wednesday 2 April

Seas and swell up so no ROV Test possible. Web down for a while so no email. Coms [communication] out. Working on expedition pics, exhibition &c [with Mike Kelly and Brian Bunge of Williamson & Assoc.]

Thursday 3 April

Swell down, lots happening readying ROV. Meetings being held. Plans being prepared. Problems with pan [camera] on ROV. ROV in midday, but @ 200m problems with TMS [Garage] preventing the ROV flying out. At 2.15 following discussions with captain/navigator/ROV [operators] and J. Perryman David went into 'teabag' [dangling the ROV alongside the wreck while still in its garage] mode. The issue now given Nigel's [N. Meikle, navigator] excellent navigation is will the cameras remain operative. 3.00PM @ 2300m?? 1510 @ stern of wreck finding it buried to the aft propeller boss … The stern buckled in with a capstan projecting mid deck. The X & Y turrets are aimed? To port and forward, the torpedo tubes are gone … The aft and fore funnel is gone as is the catapult leaving its turntable bare. Camouflage paint is visible as is the boot topping with burial to port c. @ the bilge keel … Many large holes are visible along with smaller indicating a different type of shell? … One turret aft had its roof blown off …

Friday 4 April

V. calm, Swell down 0915 ROV Repaired & back down wreck visible Back along port side redoing all from Thursday … all is going as planned … Both [David Mearns and John Perryman] now in the survey room. John logging his observations David directing & photographing stills. John read[ing] out aims. David directing the ROV operators. All filmed and observed by offwatch crew [of *Geosounder*] and self.

… The [*Sydney*] bow is fundamentally matching the break on the main wreck @ the fairlead & 7th porthole from the bow. The torpedo hit is apparent on the bow plating @ the break. The ship is buried to the bilge keels only on both sides & has only one torpedo hole. Massive number of hits by the German gunners, fires and devastation A/craft catapult, masts (lower to cheeks), HACS, Gunnery DCT, one [torpedo] tube of 4 with 2 remaining & 5 boats in amazing state … It appears the copper fastenings in the carvel hulls have prevented/slowed biological degradation though the diagonal planking on the large boat containing the smaller one appears intact.

Sunday 6 April

Description *Kormoran*

The ship is broken just @ the front of the bridge & lies on a hard bottom with bilge keels and U/W torpedo tubes visible. A small amount of sand has built up forward & there is crumpling @ the bow consistent with impact … Both bow 5.9" guns are stowed as are the torpedo tubes … the bridge has totally disintegrated. The port anchor is in place in the hawse pipe while the stbd anchor has been dismantled? & its shank lies still attached to the chain adjacent the hawsepipe on the deck … 2 [on map] two V. large sections of superstructure c. 500m distant [later measured at c. 1300m, see p 98] while 3 proved to be the flukes of the anchor embedded above visible — if it is not another anchor stowed o/b [on board].

LEFT: The collapsed quarterdeck of HMAS *Sydney*.

Australian War Memorial (David Mearns/Finding Sydney Foundation)

"I have always felt a deep dense of loss, and am keenly interested in following the recent developments on the *Sydney*, mainly for my grandchildren. I remember my late mother always seemed to find someone in the street that reminded her of him, and was never able to come to terms with his death.

"My life's wish is that the questions be answered before I die, so that we can all at last say 'goodbye'."

LESLIE MICHAEL LAWRENCE BLOM
SON OF STOKER LESLIE MICHAEL LAWRENCE BLOM

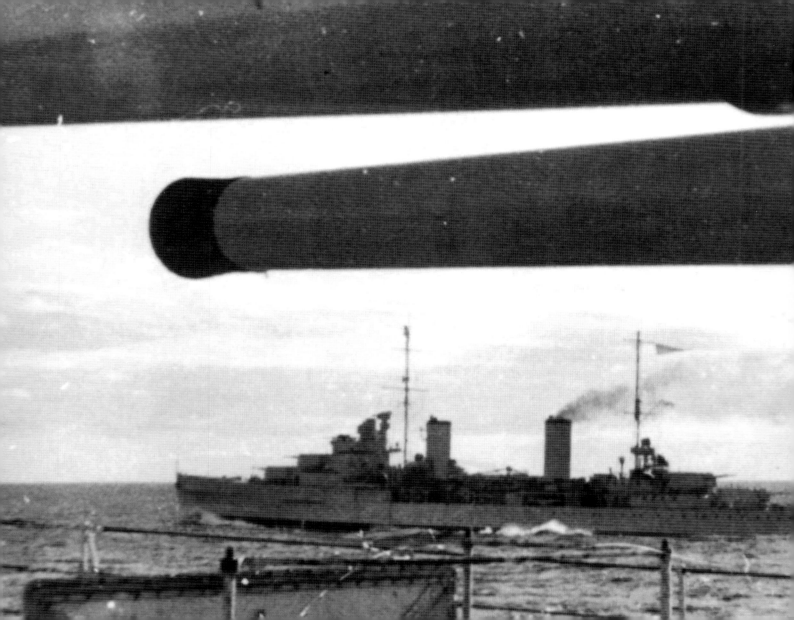

6

THE FINDINGS
OF THE COLE INQUIRY

Edited and arranged by M. McCarthy

(Source: Report of Commissioner T.R.H. Cole, 2009, *The Loss of HMAS* Sydney)[63]

On 28 March 2008, soon after the wrecks of HMAS *Sydney* and HSK *Kormoran* were found, the chief of the Australian Defence Force, Air Chief Marshal Angus Houston AC, AFC, announced the formation of a Commonwealth Defence Force Commission of Inquiry (COI) that was required to 'inquire into and report upon circumstances associated with the loss of *Sydney* in November 1941 and consequent loss of life and related events thereto'. The president was to be the Honourable Terence Cole AO RFD QC. He was given considerable procedural freedom in conducting what was to be a public inquiry. Six legal practitioners headed by Commander Jack Rush QC were appointed as counsel assisting. All were commissioned officers in the RAN Reserve or in the RAN itself.

As with earlier seminars and the 1997–98 parliamentary inquiry, the COI called for submissions and arranged to promulgate the evidence, transcripts and proceedings. There were a number of crucial differences, rendering the COI foremost above all other inquiries held earlier, including the museum's seminar, the parliamentary inquiry and the RAN Sea Power Centre's Wreck Location Seminar. The oral evidence was to be presented under oath or affirmation, and the commission had the ability to subpoena and cross-examine witnesses. None of the earlier seminars and inquiries had had this ability.

In his report the Commissioner explained his approach thus:

> *This Inquiry's objective was to provide an independent, impartial, reasoned and fact-based account of the events relating to the loss of SYDNEY ... Inevitably, I must determine a cause for the loss of SYDNEY and in doing so attribute*

responsibility … The objective of the report is to determine in an impartial way and on a reasoned basis from established facts what occurred, the circumstances in which it occurred and the consequences.

In his opening address the Commissioner acknowledged that the relatives of lost service personnel 'are entitled to assume that Australia will do all it can to establish the circumstances in which the deaths occurred'. In referring to the editor of the present volume (and thereby referencing the museum's essential contribution) as an 'early and persistent campaigner for finding *Sydney*', the Commissioner went on to note that any failure to do so would (in quoting the editor) strike 'at the heart of the notion of service to one's country and the possibility of making the ultimate sacrifice in times of dire need'.[64] The commission sat across Australia for a total of 36 days, during which it examined 77 witnesses. From the first day of sitting on 30 May 2008 to the last on 25 March 2009, the public was able to follow events, read the transcripts of evidence and cross-examination, and view images and each of the 252 exhibits on the commission's website (http://www.defence.gov.au/sydneyii/gallery. htm). In July 2009 the Commissioner produced a detailed three-volume report with transcripts of evidence, including that provided by the museum; ship's plans; visualisations of the battle by the Defence Science and Technology Organisation (DSTO) and the Royal Institution of Naval Architects (RINA); their analysis of the damage to the ships; and thirteen other appendices, a glossary and a select bibliography.[65] This was promulgated to witnesses, to those providing submissions and to those assisting in CD form. For the public the same materials appeared via the web in a manner that allowed the reader to follow what was being said,

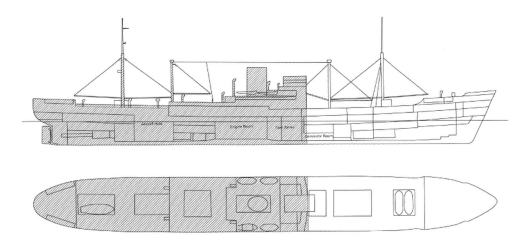

and the COI's logic in cross-examining and managing the evidence. Its footnoting system was also extensive, allowing the reader to view and download each entire reference in PDF format (http://www.defence.gov.au/sydneyii/finalreport/index. html). Many of these were 'primary sources'. This left only the unedited images from the search-and-survey phases to enter the public domain.

In November 2009, with the urging and support of the Western Australian Museum, the FSF announced that the over 1400 photographs and 50 hours of underwater video taken in the course of the investigation of the two wrecks had been donated to the Australian War Memorial. There they were to be accessioned into its collection, conserved, catalogued and made available to the public.

The Commissioner's findings

In presenting his extensive analysis — parts of which are selected and re-ordered by the editor below, but otherwise presented verbatim — in essence the Commissioner found:

The German account

- *Each of the [five WWII] interrogators independently formed the view that the groups they were interrogating were telling the truth ... That produces a high degree of probability that the general account as given is accurate ... Considerable weight is to be given to the conclusions of those experienced officers, who, as noted, each formed the view that the group they were interrogating was generally giving a truthful account of the engagement.*

Empirical [seabed] evidence

The empirical evidence supports the German account in the following respects:

- *CAPT Detmers stated that the engagement occurred at 26°S 111°E. This was verified by the finding of the wreck of SYDNEY at 26°14'45"S and 111°12'55"E and the wreck of KORMORAN at 26°06'32"S and 111°04'21"E. The wrecks are about 12 nautical miles apart.*[66]

- *The German account of the initial battle being fought with the ships on a close and parallel course about 1,000 to 1,500 metres apart is confirmed by the extent*

Western Australian crew members of
HMAS *Sydney* on deck before going
on leave, Fremantle, 1941.

West Australian Newspapers
(No Survivors: HMAS *Sydney*)

and severity of shell damage. The range of 1,000 to 1,500 metres is, in naval warfare terms, point blank. Of the at least forty-one 15-centimetre shell hits SYDNEY suffered on her port side, 34 were to the hull and superstructure of the ship, four to A turret, one to B turret and two to the catapult. Further, the flat shell trajectory, and thus close proximity between gun and target, suggested by the penetrations to the port side whaler is consistent with the German account.

- The German account of the battle has SYDNEY struck on the port side by a torpedo, about 20 metres from the bow and adjacent to A turret. This is evident in the wreck. The German account also has SYDNEY, having suffered heavy damage on her port side, falling astern after being struck by a torpedo and then turning to port, passing astern of KORMORAN and thereafter turning to starboard. KORMORAN's guns continued to fire on SYDNEY successfully, hitting her on many occasions. Of the at least forty-six 15-centimetre hits SYDNEY suffered on her starboard side, 42 hit the structure, one hit X turret, one the director control tower, one the starboard torpedo mount, and one the 4-inch gun locker. This confirms that SYDNEY must have passed astern of KORMORAN, turning to present her starboard side.

- The German account has SYDNEY's bridge and director control tower suffering severe damage early in the battle, probably resulting in the death of many officers and disrupting her firing. The underwater imagery shows there is severe damage to the bridge, the director control tower and the high-angle control station.

- The German account has the catapult hit early in the engagement, causing a *fire that destroyed the aeroplane. It is established that SYDNEY suffered two 15-centimetre port-side shell hits to the catapult.*

- *The German account has SYDNEY suffering fires that made her visible for some hours after the battle. It is now established that there was fire damage to the entire bridge structure, across the breadth of the forecastle deck, midships below the aircraft platform, across the upper deck, through the aft superstructure and upper deck on the port side, and to the aft superstructure on the starboard side below the aft control position.*

- *Some German survivors thought shell damage and fire made it unlikely that Sydney's boats would be usable. That is confirmed by observable damage to five boats found in the debris …*

The German account is that KORMORAN was scuttled, the scuttling charges causing a significant explosion of mines. The forward section of KORMORAN remains relatively intact on the seabed, but it is apparent that the aft portion of the vessel was subjected to a catastrophic explosion, causing pieces of the debris to be scattered throughout the debris field. That is consistent with the German account. So, too, is the fact that there is no observable shell fire damage to the forward section. Some German survivors said SYDNEY's shell fire did not hit the forward section.

Apart from the account of SYDNEY firing torpedoes from her starboard mounts, all the damage observable in photographs of the wrecks confirms the accuracy of the German account of the engagement and its aftermath … There is no reason to doubt the general accuracy of the German account in relation to the approach and the signals.

A badge from a public appeal, part of a national campaign to raise funds to replace the *Sydney*.

John Perryman

The sinking with no survivors

SYDNEY suffered severe damage from a torpedo hit to the forward section, about 20 metres from the bow on the port side, and incurred at least eighty-seven 15-centimetre shell hits. She was subjected to additional small-arms fire from a 3.7-centimetre gun and multiple 20-millimetre machine guns. She suffered severe fires. It can be assessed with confidence that by the time battle ceased there were many casualties on board, probably in the order of 70 percent of her complement …

> **"** *Counsel Assisting will ensure these matters are examined thoroughly and impartially, with the expectation that such review will provide the basis for a complete and objective account of the circumstances of the loss of ship and life … in the assessment of evidence … The Inquiry is inquisitorial in its nature.* **"**
>
> Commander Jack Rush[67]

It is, however, probable that there were still some alive on SYDNEY as she slowly sailed away from KORMORAN. They had available to them no lifesaving measures that would allow them to leave the ship, the observed damage pointing to a high degree of probability that all boats and Carley floats that had not been blown overboard during the battle were unserviceable because of shell and fire damage. Those who were alive when the battle ceased died when SYDNEY sank. The unknown sailor in the Carley float recovered off Christmas Island in February 1942 had suffered a serious shrapnel wound to the head, which caused his death immediately or shortly thereafter.

The sinking of a ship is violent. The force of water passing the sinking SYDNEY would have torn off the masts and rigging and dislodged loose items on the deck. Heavier items, such as funnels, the top of the bridge and the director control tower, would have soon

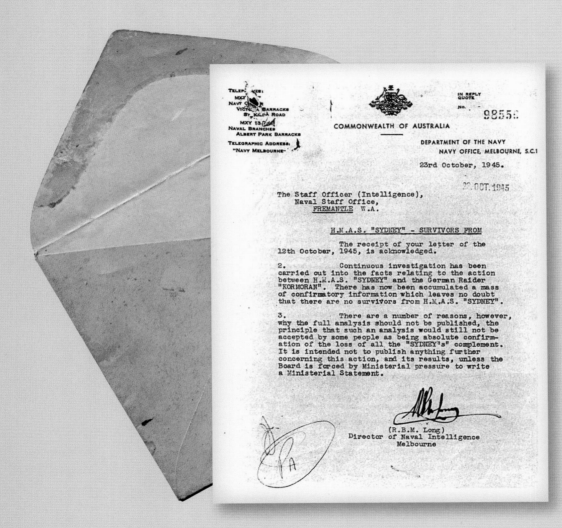

TELEPHONES:
MXY.....
NAVY OFFICE BARRACKS
ST. KILDA ROAD
MXY 1307
NAVAL BRANCHES
ALBERT PARK BARRACKS
TELEGRAPHIC ADDRESS:
"NAVY MELBOURNE"

COMMONWEALTH OF AUSTRALIA

IN REPLY
QUOTE
No. 98553

DEPARTMENT OF THE NAVY

NAVY OFFICE, MELBOURNE, S.C.1

23rd October, 1945.

29 OCT. 1945

The Staff Officer (Intelligence),
Naval Staff Office,
<u>FREMANTLE W.A.</u>

<u>H.M.A.S. "SYDNEY" - SURVIVORS FROM</u>

The receipt of your letter of the
12th October, 1945, is acknowledged.

2.   Continuous investigation has been
carried out into the facts relating to the action
between H.M.A.S. "SYDNEY" and the German Raider
"KORMORAN". There has now been accumulated a mass
of confirmatory information which leaves no doubt
that there are no survivors from H.M.A.S. "SYDNEY".

3.   There are a number of reasons, however,
why the full analysis should not be published, the
principle that such an analysis would still not be
accepted by some people as being absolute confirmation of the loss of all the "SYDNEY's" complement.
It is intended not to publish anything further
concerning this action, and its results, unless the
Board is forced by Ministerial pressure to write
a Ministerial Statement.

(R.B.M. Long)
Director of Naval Intelligence
Melbourne

The October 1945 letter confirming
the Naval Intelligence view that
there were no survivors from
HMAS *Sydney*. See pp 57–8.

Australian National Archives

followed. Boats that were still secure in their cradles would have been torn off and could have been further damaged by striking the ship or other wreckage. Very close to the surface, the force of water entering the damaged bow would have twisted and torn the bow from the ship, and in the process parts of the side shell plating, decks and bulkheads would have twisted and broken away. The differing shapes of the various pieces of wreckage would mean they sank at a speed different from the speed at which the main hull sank. Thus fittings and equipment were scattered throughout the debris field. The prospect of any crew members, particularly if they were injured, surviving that violent event was negligible.

Why did SYDNEY approach close and parallel to KORMORAN?
(Note: the following extracts are substantially re-ordered by the editor so the sequence may be more easily understood by those unfamiliar with the events.)

SYDNEY approached KORMORAN in order to identify the unknown vessel.

… Australian Squadron Tactical Note No. 9 … required the captain of the warship to make an assessment of whether the vessel 'appears innocent' or 'appears suspicious'. Two different procedures were set out — 'Case A', where the vessel 'appears innocent', and 'Case B', where the vessel 'appears suspicious'. The Case A procedure did not require the warship to go to action stations. Under Case B, however, where the vessel 'appears suspicious', the requirement was that 'if the stranger behaves in a suspicious manner or if during the approach any doubt arises as to her character, the Hands will go to Action stations'. The warship was then to stand off 7 to 8 miles from the suspicious vessel and require it to stop under threat of being fired on.

… CAPT Burnett knew there was a possibility of a raider being off the Western

Australian coast … Nonetheless, CAPT Burnett was aware of the remoteness of the possibility that the vessel sighted on 19 November 1941 was a raider.

On board the warship a 'plot' was maintained … and the vessels expected in the area, including their expected location, were shown … no ships were expected to be in the area.

… As SYDNEY approached KORMORAN from aft, her main guns were trained on KORMORAN, as were her port torpedo tubes. Her aircraft was on the catapult with the engine running … the decision to prepare it for launch can only have … been based on a doubt about whether the ship was friendly and thus there was a need to investigate it, track it to prevent its escape …

CAPT Burnett [then] assessed the sighted vessel as appearing 'innocent' … shut [the aircraft] down … did not go to action stations, and approached the vessel to 'within signalling distance' to ascertain her name.

> **" In much past literature on the loss of SYDNEY II, there has not been a sufficient distinction drawn between established fact, legitimate and justifiable deductions from such facts, and surmise. There has been much speculation and conjecture."**
>
> Commissioner T.R.H. Cole[68]

None of … five circumstances — the absence of any ship on SYDNEY's plot, the premature turn into the sun accompanied by an increase in speed, the fumbled and delayed flag signals from KORMORAN, the extended chase and the decisions to prepare to launch the Walrus and then close it down, and the Q signals — individually or cumulatively caused CAPT Burnett to amend his assessment that the ship appeared innocent.

Putting aside hindsight, as one must, it is more difficult to understand the initial

TOP: Diagram of the *Steiermark* and HSK *Kormoran* conversion.

BOTTOM: Diagram of HSK *Kormoran*, disguised as the *Straat Malakka* alongside the HMAS *Sydney* (II).

Jochen Sachse,
Western Australian Museum Collection

MeS "STEIERMARK" (Hapag, Bauj. 1938/39)

Umbau 1940

HSK 8 (Schiff 41) Hilfskreuzer "KORMORAN" (Aussehen am 19. Nov. 1941)

Die Tarnung: MS "STRAAT MALAKKA" (KPM Bau). 1939)

HMAS "SYDNEY" (Aussehen 1941)

decision to assess KORMORAN as appearing innocent when she did not appear on SYDNEY's plot … The sole empirical fact available to CAPT Burnett when making his initial decision was that the ship was not expected to be there. The terrible consequence of his erroneous decision was that SYDNEY did not go to action stations and approached to a position of great danger, where all her tactical advantages were negated and the advantage of surprise was given to KORMORAN. It resulted in the loss of SYDNEY.

Frauds, theories and speculations

… theories and speculations arose for two main reasons. The first was the absence of evidence about the engagement from an Australian perspective. The second was an unwillingness to accept that CAPT Burnett would have acted in the manner described by the German survivors …

As early as December 1941 there started to emerge a number of theories and speculations about the following:

- *Deceits engaged in by KORMORAN, some allegedly contrary to international law*

- *A conspiracy among the German survivors to tell a fabricated and inaccurate account of the engagement …*

- *Third-party involvement in the action …*

- *Various 'cover-ups' by the Australian and British Governments and Naval authorities …*

Crew carrying out maintenance on one of HMAS *Sydney*'s torpedos, Fremantle, 1941.

West Australian Newspapers
(No Survivors: HMAS *Sydney*)

... A number of commentators have theorised that HSK KORMORAN ... stopped on an order from SYDNEY ... knew and used STRAAT MALAKKA's secret call sign ... or ... engaged in an illegal ruse de guerre or other trick to lure HMAS SYDNEY into ... close proximity ... [including] flying a Norwegian flag ... pretended to surrender ... feigned an engineering or medical emergency ... emitted a smoke screen ...

None of the theories or speculations advanced by the authors referred to explains why SYDNEY approached so close to KORMORAN ... KORMORAN did not fly a ... Norwegian [or] white flag or otherwise surrender or indicate she was surrendering. The German account of the engagement makes that clear ... There is no evidence at all to support the speculation that KORMORAN signalled that she had suffered a mechanical or medical emergency ... or create a smoke screen. No one on board KORMORAN ever suggested she did ... KORMORAN did not stop on any order from SYDNEY ... SYDNEY did not lower a boat for the purpose of investigating or boarding KORMORAN, nor was she preparing to do so. There is no doubt that KORMORAN did not have STRAAT MALAKKA's secret call sign.

... The theories have been advanced in an attempt to find an explanation for the approach that would exculpate CAPT Burnett by establishing conduct on the part of KORMORAN and CAPT Detmers that was in breach of international law or was otherwise an impermissible ruse de guerre. When examined, not one of the theories advanced has any substance.

PAGE 133

Sailors and embarked soldiers in one of *Sydney's* mess decks, 1940.

Sea Power Centre–Australia

"After the war we never mentioned Charlie's name. The family grieved for him and hoped he would return from a POW camp. It was strange because there was this feeling it would upset Mum to talk about the subject ...

"This is one reason why I feel a search by the government is necessary, just to put to rest the grieving after all this time. It would let them know what happened to their loved ones all those years ago."

JUNE BICKLE
SISTER OF ORDINARY SEAMAN 2ND CLASS CHARLES WILLIAM PATRICK

7

MANAGING THE WRECKS

Ross Anderson,[69] M. McCarthy and Andrew Viduka[70]

Protection before finding

It is important to note that both HMAS *Sydney* and HSK *Kormoran* as warships remain the property of their respective national governments, having been neither captured nor surrendered. As defined by one commentator

> *Warships, naval auxiliaries, and other vessels owned or operated by a State and used at the time they sank only on government non-commercial service, are State vessels. Aircraft used in military, customs and police services are State aircraft. International law recognises that State vessels and aircraft, and their associated artefacts, whether or not sunken, are entitled to sovereign immunity.*[71]

The seagull dome. HMAS Sydney II Memorial, Geraldton.

Western Australian Museum (Jon Carpenter)

As with all shipwrecks in Australian waters, the primary recognition and protection for sites deemed historic is provided under the terms of the Commonwealth *Historic Shipwrecks Act 1976* (the Act). Administration of the Act is carried out by the minister responsible, in conjunction with officers in the Maritime Heritage Section, Heritage Division within the Department of the Environment, Water, Heritage and the Arts (DEWHA). Each Australian state, the Northern Territory and Norfolk Island has a minister's delegate appointed to undertake certain sections of the Act to facilitate day-to-day administration. In Western Australia, the minister's delegate is the Chief Executive Officer of the Western Australian Museum.

Western Australian Museum involvement with the *Sydney* and *Kormoran* commenced after 1981 with the first indications that *Sydney* may have been found (see chapter on the search above). As indicated earlier, considerable amounts of time, facilities and expertise, together with Commonwealth historic shipwreck funds, were expended by the Western Australian Museum's Department of Maritime Archaeology in attending to the Museum CEO's brief as the delegate to the minister responsible for the operations of the Act.

After the operations of the Act were extensively reviewed in 1990, the Act was amended in 1993 to include section 4A, allowing for the blanket protection of all shipwrecks that were at least 75 years old and their associated relics. Though there remained provision for the declaration of more modern wrecks, the 75-year blanket protection, rolling-date provision became the primary criterion for declaration.

In mid 2001 in the lead up to the 2001 Sea Power Centre Finding Sydney seminar, clarification was sought as to the status of the then unfound *Sydney* and *Kormoran* wrecks in the context of these legislative changes. Advice was received from Environment Australia (the then department responsible for administering the Act) that these two wrecks could only be declared historic under the Act when their location became known, or where there was reasonable evidence to believe that the remains lay in Australian waters or in waters above its continental shelf. In receiving a request from the museum for clarification on this advice, the then minister replied that while there 'was some evidence for the final location of *Kormoran*, there is considerable dispute as to where *Sydney* may have eventually sunk'. On that basis he also advised that while he was certainly prepared to make a provisional declaration of Historic Shipwrecks under section 6 of the Act, he was unable to act until the wrecks were found. In closing, however, the minister observed, however, that

Looking out to sea from the HMAS Sydney II Memorial, Geraldton.

Western Australian Museum (Jon Carpenter)

The grave of the unknown HMAS *Sydney* seaman washed ashore at Christmas Island, Geraldton War Cemetery.[72]

Western Australian Museum (Ross Anderson)

I appreciate the considerable effort that the Museum has contributed on the Commonwealth's behalf … [and] I would be grateful if you could, as my Delegate under this legislation, continue to monitor and advise on any progress in locating the remains of these vessels.[73]

Protective measure post-finding

When the wrecks were believed located in Australian waters a provisional declaration as Historic Shipwrecks was immediately declared by the Minister, the Honourable Peter Garrett. Following the ROV images which provided conclusive identification of the two wrecks, the way was then clear for a final declaration. Subsequently on 19 November 2008, the 67th anniversary of the battle between *Sydney* and *Kormoran*, the Minister declared the wrecks and their associated relics to be historic shipwrecks, with associated protected zones. Other World War II shipwrecks that have been specifically declared historic in Australia include SS *Florence D* (1942) and the Japanese submarine IJN *I–124* (1942) in the Northern Territory, the Japanese midget submarine IJN *M–24* (1942) and SS *Iron Knight* (1943) in New South Wales and AHS *Centaur* (1943) in Queensland (the subject of another successful search led by David Mearns) and MV *City of Rayville* (1940) in Victoria. SMS *Emden*, which was defeated by HMAS *Sydney* (I) in World War I at the Cocos (Keeling) Islands, lies in Australian waters and it too has been declared historic (see page 16).

While the great depth of the *Sydney* and *Kormoran* sites precludes scuba diving,

The Stele at the HMAS Sydney II Memorial.

Western Australian Museum (Jon Carpenter)

human interference is still possible via jettisoning or dumping of intrusive modern material onto the sites, subsea operations, and interference with or removal of material from the sites by ROVs. As the delegated manager for the *Sydney* and *Kormoran* sites, the museum will continue to work in cooperation with the Australian Government to ensure the sites are protected in perpetuity in accordance with the world's best-practice guidelines for the protection of underwater cultural heritage sites. These guidelines are defined in the annex to the UNESCO 2001 Convention on the Protection of the Underwater Cultural Heritage. This has as its objectives the in-situ preservation of underwater cultural heritage sites, and the banning of commercial exploitation of historic shipwrecks and their relics.[74]

The Western Australian Museum will in the near future be working with DEWHA, the German Embassy and RAN on developing appropriate management plans for both these sites. The primary aim of future management will be to ensure that the sites are not disturbed, will not have material removed from them, and that intrusive modern material is not deposited on the sites. For example, cruise ships and naval vessels wishing to enter the protected zones around each wreck to lay wreaths in waters above the sites will be requested to ensure that all materials are biodegradable. In responding to their applications for entry to the zones, cruise operators are advised of the memorials at Carnarvon where the German sailors came ashore, of the evocative HMAS *Sydney* Memorial at Geraldton, and the nearby Commonwealth War Graves Commission (CWGC) Geraldton War Cemetery where the 'Unknown Sailor' from Christmas Island now lies. The Western Australian Museum's exhibits and education programs at Geraldton and Fremantle, as well as its special website

(http://www.museum.wa.gov.au/sydney), are other features. By commemorating the lost men, these programs are designed to add to the Australian War Memorial's exhibits and websites, to the Naval Association of Australia and Finding Sydney Foundation's web-based Virtual Memorial (www.sydneymemorial.com) and to the RAN's Sea Power Centre's historical data and honour rolls.

Wartime shipwreck sites are often incorrectly described as 'war graves'. However, this term has a very specific definition according to the CWGC, which is responsible for commemoration of Commonwealth war dead of the two world wars, and cannot be used other than for the official commemoration by interment of remains of our Commonwealth war dead in an established grave with a regulation headstone. In instances whereby remains from the two world wars are recovered today, they are buried in the nearest practicable war cemetery in a 'war grave'. Thus the remains of the 'Unknown Sailor' from Christmas Island were re-interred, at the Geraldton War Cemetery, after forensic tests proved he was from *Sydney*.

> *"Human beings have difficulty in living with the unknown, and they are even more uncomfortable with the unknowable. The seas are probably the world's largest store of both the unknown and the unknowable."*
>
> Tom Frame[75]

While the CWGC commemorates all Commonwealth casualties from the two world wars, it is not always possible to commemorate them in a war grave. After World War I it was necessary to find an appropriate way of commemorating those members of the Royal Navy (and Royal Australian Navy) who died at sea and had no known grave. Permanent memorials could not be provided where ships were lost, so it was decided that identical memorials should be built at each of the three manning ports in Great Britain: Chatham, Plymouth and Portsmouth. Generally the names of those missing at sea are listed on one of these memorials. Casualties of the RAN, including those from the *Sydney*, are commemorated on the Plymouth Memorial. The Tower Hill Memorial in London is dedicated to those who lost their lives serving in the merchant navy and fishing fleets. Similarly, those who lost their lives in the Air Force are commemorated on the memorial at Runnymede in Surrey.

Contemporary practice to commemorate military and civilian maritime losses during war has also included the construction of memorials on shore, in similar fashion to the many land-based memorials commemorating significant battles on land. In the case of HMAS *Sydney* and HSK *Kormoran*, protected zones were also declared under the *Historic Shipwrecks Act* to ensure effective protection for any remains entombed within vessels.

PAGE 145

HMAS *Sydney* in Geraldton, Western Australia, October 1941.

Geraldton Guardian

"The family was devastated. His son was thirteen at the time, and Mum had to be the breadwinner and never remarried. Her ashes were scattered off the coast where *Sydney* was lost; that was her last wish."

J.A. MCLEOD-SMITH
SON OF CHIEF PETTY OFFICER ALBERT FRASER MCLEOD-SMITH

VISIT: WWW.MUSEUM.WA.GOV.AU/SYDNEY

PROTECTING AUSTRALIA'S MARITIME HERITAGE

Australia has a long, rich and diverse maritime history. From the earliest known shipwreck, the *Trial*, in 1622 to the recent discovery of HMAS *Sydney* and HSK *Kormoran,* thousands of ships have sunk in Australian waters and been re-discovered.

To ensure that shipwrecks — underwater for at least 75 years or specifically declared by the Minister — are protected, the Australian Government introduced the Historic Shipwreck Act in 1976. This legislation protects the physical remains of shipwrecks and their associated relics.

The Australian Government Department of the Environment, Water, Heritage and the Arts is responsible for the administration of the *Historic Shipwreck Act 1976* and works cooperatively with the states, the Northern Territory and Norfolk Island to ensure our shipwreck heritage is protected and conserved, now and for future generations.

As well as the Historic Shipwrecks Act, in 1992 the Government established the Historic Shipwrecks Program (HSP). This program was introduced to increase the knowledge, use, appreciation and enjoyment of Australia's historic shipwrecks by funding projects that conserve, protect and preserve wrecks and their associated relics.

Projects funded under the HSP include the excavations of the First Fleet's flagship HMS *Sirius* (1790) at Norfolk Island, HMS *Pandora* (1791) in Queensland, *Batavia* (1629) in Western Australia, *Clonmel* (1841) in Victoria and *Sydney Cove* (1797) in Tasmania. Other significant projects include the protection of the Japanese Submarine IJN *I-124* (1942) in the Northern Territory, the Japanese midget submarine *M-24* (1942) in New South Wales, SS *Admella* (1859) in South Australia and ongoing management of Australia's most popular historic shipwreck dive site, the SS *Yongala* (1911) in Queensland.

Importantly, while this program is focused on the protection and conservation of shipwrecks, it is not at the exclusion of people experiencing Australia's maritime heritage. Indeed, the program has long focused on encouraging responsible recreational diving as well as encouraging community participation in locating, documenting, monitoring and protecting shipwrecks. The HSP ensures that Australia's historic shipwreck heritage continues to be accessible and valued, now and into the future.

For more information about Australia's maritime heritage please visit:

www.environment.gov.au/heritage/shipwrecks

ENDNOTES

1   Collins, Vice Admiral Sir J. (1971). *HMAS* Sydney, Naval Historical Society of Australia, Garden Island, Sydney. Sea Power Centre — Australia (SPC-A). Ship histories website. http://www.navy.gov.au/HMAS_Sydney_(II). With advice and assistance from Lt D.J. Perryman (RANR, CSM), senior naval historical officer, SPC-A.

2   Ross, W.H. (1946). *Stormy Petrel: The Life Story of HMAS* Sydney, chapter 5, '*Sydney* v. *Colleoni* and *Bande Nere*'. Patersons Printing Press, Perth: 16.

3   A yard of 36 inches was common usage in gunnery throughout the period covered in this work. With the distances quoted all being approximate and a metre being 39.37 inches, a rough 1:1 conversion can be made. In this instance the distance was c. 20,000 metres.

4   In Collins, J. (1971). *HMAS* Sydney. Naval Historical Society of Australia, Garden Island, NSW: 20.

5   Collins op. cit.

6   SPC-A website op. cit., with advice and assistance from Lt. D.J. Perryman (Fn 1 above) Capt. Peter Hore (RN retd), Wes Olson and Barbara Poniewierski (Winter), authors and researchers (see references to their works below).

7   Summerell, R. (1997). *The Sinking of HMAS* Sydney: *A Guide to Commonwealth Government Records*. Australian Archives, Canberra: 12.

8   Detmers, T.A. (1959). *The Raider* Kormoran. William Kimber, London.

9   Winter, B. (1984). *HMAS* Sydney: *Fact, Fantasy & Fraud*. Booralong Press, Boolarong, Queensland. Also B. Poniewierski to M. McCarthy, pers. comm., 13/11/2009.

10 McCarthy, M. (2008). 'An insight into the genesis and evolution of the HMAS *Sydney* controversy.' Prepared for the HMAS *Sydney* II Commission of Inquiry. Western Australian Museum, Department of Maritime Archaeology, Report No 243. http://www.defence.gov.au/sydneyii/WAM/WAM.070.0010.pdf. Based on entries to WA Museum, Department of Maritime Archaeology file 630/81 Nos. 1–56. HMAS *Sydney*/HSK *Kormoran*.

11 Navy Office. Copy of Message. From S.O. Wellington to HMS *Achilles*, HMS *Leander*, Naval Officer Suva 28/11/1941. Source SPC-A.

12 Reproduced in Summerell R. (1999). *Sinking of HMAS* Sydney: *A Guide to Commonwealth Government Records* (3rd edn). Australian Archives, Canberra: 16.

13 Robotham, J. (nd). *Eagle in the Crow's Nest* (ms copy held by State Library of Western Australia).

14 The Commonwealth Government's shipwrecks unit at this time was within the Department of Home Affairs. It has undergone many name and staff changes since 1976. Presently it is within the Department of the Environment, Water, Heritage and the Arts (DEWHA).

15 WA Museum, Department of Maritime Archaeology. HMAS *Sydney*/HSK *Kormoran* file, 630/81 vols. 2–5.

16 Montgomery, M. (1981). *Who Sank the* Sydney? Cassell, Melbourne.

17 Detmers, op. cit.

18 Winter, op. cit.

19 McCarthy, M. (2008). 'A précis of search-related events leading up to the commencement of the HMAS Sydney Search.' The basis of a

speech presented at the announcement of the HMAS *Sydney* search in November 2007 at the Western Australian Maritime Museum. Western Australian Museum, Department of Maritime Archaeology, Report No 230. Based on entries to WA Museum, Department of Maritime Archaeology file 630/81 Nos. 1–56. HMAS *Sydney*/HSK *Kormoran*. The files were kindly indexed gratis by Dr John McArthur assisted by Susan Cox.

20 Green, J., McCarthy, M. and Penrose, J. (1984). 'Site inspection by remote sensing: The HMAS *Sydney* search: A case study'. *The Bulletin of the Australian Institute for Maritime Archaeology*, 8(1): 24–42

21 Over the years these companies were incorporated into other entities. Principals were J. Cuneen, G. Glazier, T. Graham, G. Reudavey, T. Ridsell-Smith and G. Roughan.

22 Western Australian Museum, HMAS *Sydney* File, 630–81, 04/01/91: 114–8.

23 McCarthy, M. & Kirsner, K. (comp) (1992). Papers from the HMAS *Sydney* Forum, Fremantle 21–23 November, 1991. Report — Department of Maritime Archaeology, No. 52. Given the conflicting nature of the historical and oral data, though also appearing in this work, they were not factored in to the oceanographic analyses.

24 Detmers, op. cit.

25 Kirsner, K. & Hughes, S. (1993). 'HMAS *Sydney* and HSK *Kormoran*: Possible and probable search areas.' Report, Department of Maritime Archaeology, Western Australian Maritime Museum, No. 71, November 1993.

26 Ibid. McCarthy and Kirsner op. cit. The many researchers and attendees appear listed in that compilation.

27 Olson, W. (1995). 'HMAS *Sydney* (1934–1941): Possible and probable cause of her loss.' Report, Department of Maritime Archaeology, No. 104, WA Maritime Museum, Fremantle. Olson (1996). 'With all hands: A study of the circumstances surrounding the loss of the 645 officers and men aboard HMAS *Sydney* in November 1941.' Report No. 116, Department of Maritime Archaeology, WA Maritime Museum, Fremantle.

28 Olson W. (2000). *Bitter Victory: The Death of HMAS* Sydney (2nd edn). University of Western Australia Press, Perth.

29 Those honoured by the museum for their HMAS *Sydney* and other related work were Ted Graham, Kim Kirsner , Ed Punchard and Wes Olson.

30 For example, McDonald G., (2005). *Seeking the* Sydney: *A Quest for Truth*. University of Western Australia Press, Perth.

31 T. Graham notes that in providing advice to the HMAS Sydney Foundation Trust, 'Rear Admiral Holthouse (RAN), an engineer with combat experience, advised them that it was extremely unlikely that HMAS *Sydney* could have reached the Abrolhos <u>and</u> failed to transit a signal <u>and</u> failed [his emphasis] to yield any survivors'. Kim Kirsner also advised that his 1997 research 'demonstrated that the observations of the *Kormoran* survivors were consistent with the assumption that the cruiser rapidly lost way after the battle' (pers. comm. T. Graham to McCarthy 3/11/2009). Conversely Wes Olson's Archival Committee of the 2001 SPC Seminar (which included Capt. Peter Hore (RN retd) concluded that while they believed it lay close to *Kormoran*, *Sydney* 'might have stayed afloat for a considerably longer period than the German statements suggest' and that it could lie 'up to one hundred nautical miles SSE of position 26°South 111° East' (2001: 52).

32 For Dowsing see http://www.dowsingworks.com/id42.html. For KDLS see Whitakker, T., and Knight L., 2001. 'The search for the wrecks of HMAS *Sydney* and HSK *Kormoran* in 1989, 1998, 2001 using the Knight Direct Location System.' In McCarthy, M. (comp.) (2002). 'Submissions to the HMAS *Sydney* II Seminar.' Report, Department of Maritime Archaeology, Western Australian Maritime Museum, No. 164: 132p.

33 Report of the 1997–98 parliamentary inquiry, quoting the Western Australian Museum submission:148.

34 Joint Standing Committee on Foreign Affairs, Defence and Trade (1999). Report on the loss of HMAS *Sydney*, Parliament of the Commonwealth of Australia, Canberra. Though the proceedings of the earlier Geraldton (G. McDonald, convenor) and Fremantle (J. Doohan, convenor) forums were not published, details of their content and their effect in the lead-up to the parliamentary inquiry appear in McDonald, G., op. cit., Chapter 10. 'HMAS *Sydney* Forums and Other Leads'.

35 Hore P. (2001). *HMAS* Sydney: *The Cruiser and the Controversy in the Archives of the United Kingdom.* Royal Australian Navy Sea Power Centre, Canberra.

36 Royal Australian Navy Sea Power Centre. 'HMAS *Sydney* II.' Proceedings of the Wreck Location Seminar, 16 November 2001. Department of Defence, Canberra.

37 McCarthy, M., (comp.) (2002). 'Submissions to the HMAS *Sydney* II seminar.' Report, Department of Maritime Archaeology. Western Australian Maritime Museum, No. 164.

38 Prof. Peter Dennis (2001). HMAS *Sydney* Wreck seminar — Closing Remarks (SPC) — 2001 Wreck Location Seminar, op. cit.

39 Political support was provided by MPs P. Filing, I. MacLean, G. Edwards and S. Smith. As its first project, the trust sought to have an anomaly located in c. 100 metres of water SW of Carnarvon examined. Though the museum and the RAN indicated they were committed to examining the site in due course, convinced it was very significant the trust elected to proceed independently. After obtaining sponsorship from the *West Australian* newspaper, a team led by Mr Born, including the finder, Mr Edwards, and Ted Graham set out to examine it the following May. The subsequent news item advising of the failure to locate a wreck also ominously noted that in the terrible weather encountered on site, 'most members of the party had become very sick — Mr Born very ill'. Though he recovered from the combined effects of seasickness and a virus sufficiently to conduct an interview with the *West Australian*, not long after that Mr Born died of heart failure.

40 http://www.prospero.com.au/about/. The film was co-produced by Julia Redwood.

41 The many politicians and patrons involved are listed in McCarthy, 2008, op. cit. http://www.museum.wa.gov.au/collections/maritime/march/documents/No._230_Sydney_search_chronology.pdf

42 The list of supporters appears in McCarthy, 2008, op. cit.

43 Their position was 25°58'S 110°56'E. This is rounded to 26°S 111°E for ease of understanding.

44 Sea Power Centre, op. cit: 52. The committee comprised Wes Olson, Capt. Peter Hore, CMDR Geoff Vickridge (RFD RANR Retd.) and Richard Goldsmith.

45 T. Graham and K. Kirsner to M. McCarthy, pers. comms., 2–5/11/2009.

Reproducing in Graham's case excerpts from a 'Proposed 2005 Search' distributed by him on 30 May 2005 to members of the Technical Search Committee of the FSF and to D. Mearns. In it Kirsner and Dunn had identified a 45 x 30 km search area for the *Kormoran* centred on a presumed sinking position at 26°4'S 111°2'E. [here rounded to 26°S 111°E]. They also deduced that *Sydney* lay in the SE quadrant from there. According to Kirsner, he and Dunn had demonstrated that the *Kormoran* survivors' accounts 'were consistent with Frequency Distribution referred to as Zipf's Law (see reference list) a distribution that describes a wide variety of natural phenomena, including language production and memory'. This was also explained as a 'mathematical decision model to integrate information from reports from the survivors' to produce a 'small search area that included *Kormoran*. Details appear in Kirsner, K., and Dunn, J., 2004. *Search for HSK* Kormoran *and HMAS* Sydney *II: A Cognitive Perspective*. Produced for the FSF and promulgated to the web in 2005. http://www.whereissydney.com/

46   D. Mearns to M. McCarthy, pers. comm., 29/10/09. He advises that 'key to the Government's decision to fund a search was the RAN's reversal of their official position not to support a search. I, and the FSF, independently lobbied the RAN Chief Ritchie and it was the re-discovery and analysis of Detmers' dictionary by Mearns & Peter Hore that changed Ritchie's opinion. This chronology is detailed in my book'. See Mearns, 2009, following.

47   He resigned on 15 November 2004. Bob King resigned on 1 June 2006 and Ron Birmingham left on 5 October 2006. Though departing prematurely, their contributions were all essential to the final success.

48   HMAS Sydney Search Pty Ltd. 'The search to find and identify the wrecks of HMAS *Sydney* II and HSK *Kormoran*.' Final report, Finding Sydney Search Foundation, Perth: 2–3. http://presspass.findingsydney.com/blogs/official_finding_sydney_foundation_media_releases/archive/2008/10/28/report.aspx

49   The were local and overseas firms Agip, ROC Oil, Apache Northwest, Voyager Energy and Bounty Oil and Gas.

50   Dr A. Lockwood to M. McCarthy pers. comm., 16/09/02 advising that on 11 September 2001 he had sent a damning review of the KDLS system to the history unit, RAN. HMAS *Sydney* File 630–81–39 & 42

51   That speech is the basis for this chapter. McCarthy op. cit., 2008.

52   FSF, 2008. Final report op. cit.; Mearns, D. (2009). *The Search for the* Sydney*: How Australia's Greatest Maritime Mystery Was Solved*. Harper Collins, Sydney. Perryman, D. J. (2008). Report on the search for the wrecks of HMAS *Sydney* & HSK *Kormoran*. February–April 2008. Royal Australian Navy Sea Power Centre; WA Museum, HMAS *Sydney*/HSK *Kormoran* wreck inspection daybook.

53   Mearns explains his reasons for doing so in his book. op. cit.: 104–5.

54   Hore P. (2009). Sydney*: Cipher and Search: Solving the Last Great Naval Mystery of the Second World War*. Seafarer Books, Suffolk, UK.

55   ibid.: 20.

56   The process is described in Mearns, op. cit.: 127–131.

57   The position provided for *Kormoran* in the FSF Report and by Commissioner Cole is 26°06'32"S 111°04'21"E. DEWHA uses 26°05'57"S 111°04'24"E. David Mearns, op. cit: 149 provides 26° 05'46"S 111°04'33"E as the centre of a large oval-shaped debris field measuring nearly one kilometre across. Being the location of the explosion that followed the scuttling, it lies in between the forward

half of *Kormoran,* which is located c. 1300 metres away from the second largest piece of wreckage, possibly the remains of the engine and superstructure. Each authority is fixing on different features.

58 FSF Report op. cit.: vi

59 The position provided for *Sydney* in the FSF Report and by Commissioner Cole is 26°14'45"S 111°12'55"E. David Mearns uses 26°14'31"S 111°12'48"E. DEWHA uses 26°14'39"S 111°12'48"S. Again it lies in a large debris field with each authority fixing on different features.

60 Olson's 2001 team had centred on 25°58'S 110°56'E, with *Sydney* possibly lying within 15NM. Kirsner and Dunn fixed *Kormoran* at 26°4'S 111°2'E, with *Sydney* lying in the SE quandrant nearby.

61 Detmers, op. cit.: 147–8.

62 The Williamson team, the DOF Subsea ROV operators, the ship's crew and the specialist support staff are all listed in the FSF Report. Project manager was Patrick Flynn.

63 Commissioner T.R.H. Cole, 2009. *The Loss of HMAS* Sydney. Available in CD and on the web. http://www.defence.gov.au/sydneyii/finalreport/index.html

64 Commissioner T.R.H. Cole, 2008, opening statement, Commission of Inquiry into the loss of HMAS *Sydney* II: 2–3.

65 DSTO and RINA also produced a hard copy (with CD) of their report. Australian Government Department of Defence, Defence Science and Technology Organisation & the Royal Institution of Naval Architects, 2009. HMAS *Sydney* II Commission of Inquiry: Report on technical aspects of the sinking of HMAS *Sydney* and HSK *Kormoran*. Maritime Platforms Division, DSTO, Fishermans Bend Victoria.

66 See endnote 57 and 69.

67 Commander Jack Rush on being granted Leave to Appear before the Commission of Inquiry. Cole, 2008: 10–11.

68 Commissioner T.R.H. Cole, 2008, opening statement, Commission of Inquiry into the loss of HMAS *Sydney* II: 4.

69 Maritime Archaeology Department, WA Museum, President, the Australasian Institute for Maritime Archaeology.

70 Assistant Director, Maritime Heritage Section, Historic Heritage Branch, Heritage Division, Department of Environment, Water, Heritage and the Arts.

71 Roach, J.A. (1996). 'Sunken warships and military aircraft.' *Marine Policy*, Vol. 20 Issue 4: 351.

72 The use of the words 'A Serviceman' on the headstone evidently allows for the possibility that the Unknown Sailor was an officer, seaman, an airman, a steward or other serviceman posted to HMAS *Sydney*. For the an account of the Christmas Island burial and the location of the grave read Ted McGowan's and Glenys McDonald's accounts: http://www.hmassydney.com/australiasforgottenson.html and http://www.hmassydney.com/christmasisland.html

73 Dr D. Kemp, Minister for the Environment and Heritage, to G. Henderson, Delegate. 18/06/02. HMAS Sydney File 630/81 Vol. 42: 103–4.

74 http://unesdoc.unesco.org/images/0012/001260/126065e.pdf

75 Frame, T. (2008). *HMAS* Sydney: *Loss and Controversy*. Hachette Livre, Sydney: vi. This work was first produced as one of the recommendations of the Museum's 1991 Seminar.

BIBLIOGRAPHY

Australian Government Department of Defence, Defence Science and Technology Organisation and the Royal Institution of Naval Architects, 2009, HMAS *Sydney* II Commission of Inquiry. 'Report on technical aspects of the sinking of HMAS *Sydney* and HSK *Kormoran*.' Maritime Platforms Division, DSTO, Fishermans Bend, Victoria.

Australia International Council on Monuments and Sites (ICOMOS) Burra Charter, 1988.

Cole, Commissioner T.R.H. (2009). *The Loss of HMAS* Sydney *II*. Department of Defence, Canberra.

Collins, Vice Admiral Sir J (1971). *HMAS* Sydney. Naval Historical Society of Australia, Garden Island, Sydney.

Detmers, T.A. (1959). *The Raider* Kormoran. William Kimber, London.

Frame, T. (2008). *HMAS* Sydney: *Australia's Greatest Naval Tragedy*. Hachette Australia.

Green, J., McCarthy, M. and Penrose, J. (1984). 'Site inspection by remote sensing: The HMAS *Sydney* search: A case study'. *The Bulletin of the Australian Institute for Maritime Archaeology* 8(1): 24–42.

HMAS Sydney Search Pty Ltd. 'Final report: The search to find and identify the wrecks of HMAS *Sydney* II and HSK *Kormoran*.' Finding Sydney Foundation, Perth: 2–3. http://presspass.findingsydney. com/blogs/official_finding_sydney_foundation_media_releases/ archive/2008/10/28/report.aspx.

Hore P. (2001). *HMAS* Sydney: *The Cruiser and the Controversy in the Archives of the United Kingdom*. Royal Australian Navy Sea Power Centre, Canberra.

Hore P. (2009). Sydney: *Cipher and Search: Solving the Last Great Naval Mystery of the Second World War*. Seafarer Books, Suffolk, UK.

Hoyt, E.P. (1967). *The Last Cruise of the* Emden. Andre Deutsch, London.

Joint Standing Committee on Foreign Affairs, Defence and Trade (1999). 'Report on the Loss of HMAS *Sydney*.' Parliament of the Commonwealth of Australia, Canberra.

Kirsner, K. and Dunn, J.C. (2004). 'The search for HSK *Kormoran* and HMAS *Sydney* II: A cognitive perspective.' The University of Western Australia site for the Cognitive Analysis of Archival, Historical and Memory Databases. http://www.whereissydney.com/

Kirsner, K. and Dunn, J.C. (2008). 'Search definition in the search for *Kormoran* and *Sydney*: Triumph for cognitive science.' Cole Commission of Inquiry. http://www.defence.gov.au/sydneyii/ transcripts.htm. HMAS *Sydney* II Commission of Inquiry: Submissions (04/11/2008, SUBM.006.0222).

Kirsner, K., and Hughes, S. (1993). 'HMAS *Sydney* and HSK *Kormoran*: Possible and probable search areas.' Report, Department of Maritime Archaeology, Western Australian Maritime Museum, No. 71, November 1993.

McCarthy, M. (2008). 'An insight into the genesis and evolution of the HMAS *Sydney* controversy.' Prepared for the HMAS *Sydney* II Commission of Inquiry. Western Australian Museum, Department of Maritime Archaeology, Report No. 243. http://www.defence.gov. au/sydneyii/WAM/WAM.070.0010.pdf. Based on entries to WA Museum, Department of Maritime Archaeology file 630/81 Nos. 1–56. HMAS *Sydney*/HSK *Kormoran*.

McCarthy, M. and Kirsner, K. (comp.) (1992). 'Papers from the HMAS *Sydney* forum, Fremantle 21–23 November, 1991.' Report, Department of Maritime Archaeology, No. 52.

McCarthy, M., (comp.) (2002). 'Submissions to the HMAS *Sydney* II seminar.' Report, Department of Maritime Archaeology. Western Australian Maritime Museum, No. 164.

McCarthy, M. (2008). 'A précis of search-related events leading up to the commencement of the HMAS *Sydney* Search.' The basis of a speech presented at the announcement of the HMAS *Sydney* search in November 2007 at the Western Australian Maritime Museum. Western Australian Museum, Department of Maritime Archaeology, Report No 230. Based on entries to WA Museum, Department of Maritime Archaeology file 630/81 Nos. 1–56. HMAS *Sydney*/HSK *Kormoran*. http://www.museum.wa.gov.au/collections/maritime/march/documents/No._230_Sydney_search_chronology.pdf.

McDonald G. (2005). *Seeking the* Sydney: *A Quest for Truth*. University of Western Australia Press, Perth.

Mearns, D. (2009). *The Search for the* Sydney: *How Australia's Greatest Maritime Mystery Was Solved*. Harper Collins, Sydney.

Montgomery, M. (1981). *Who Sank the* Sydney? Cassell, Melbourne & Penguin.

Olson, W. (1995). 'HMAS *Sydney* (1934–1941): Possible and probable cause of her loss.' Report, Department of Maritime Archaeology, No 104. WA Maritime Museum, Fremantle.

Olson, W. (1996). 'With all hands: A study of the circumstances surrounding the loss of the 645 officers and men aboard HMAS *Sydney* in November 1941'. Report No. 116, Department of Maritime Archaeology, WA Maritime Museum, Fremantle.

Olson, W. (2000). *Bitter Victory: The Death of HMAS* Sydney (2nd edn). University of Western Australia Press, Perth.

Perryman, D. J. (2008). 'Report on the search for the wrecks of HMAS *Sydney* & HSK *Kormoran*, February–April 2008.' Royal Australian Navy Sea Power Centre.

Robotham, J. (nd). *Eagle in the Crow's Nest* (ms copy held by State Library of Western Australia).

Roach, J.A. (1996) 'Sunken warships and military aircraft.' *Marine Policy*, Vol. 20 Issue 4: 351.

Ross, W.H. (1943). *Stormy Petrel: The Life Story of HMAS* Sydney. Patersons, Perth.

Ross, W.H. (1994). *Lucky Ross: An R.A.N. Officer 1934–1951*. Hesperian, Perth.

Royal Australian Navy, Sea Power Centre (SPC). 'HMAS *Sydney* II: Proceedings of the Wreck Location Seminar, 16 November 2001.' Department of Defence, Canberra.

Sea Power Centre — Australia (SPC-A) Ship histories website. http://www.navy.gov.au/HMAS_Sydney_(II).

Shegog, K. (2002). *Lost But Not Forgotten: A Bitter Sweet Victory: HMAS* Sydney *II: In Memory of the 645*. Single X Publications, Glenside, SA.

Summerell, R. (1999). *Sinking of HMAS* Sydney: *A Guide to Commonwealth Government Records* (3rd edn). Australian Archives, Canberra.

Western Australian Museum, Department of Maritime Archaeology. HMAS *Sydney*/HSK *Kormoran* file, 630/81 1–56.

Western Australian Museum. HMAS *Sydney*/HSK *Kormoran* wreck inspection daybook.

Winter, B. (1984). *HMAS* Sydney: *Fact, Fantasy & Fraud*. Booralong Press, Brisbane.

Zipf, G.K. (1935). *The Psychobiology of Language*. Houghton-Mifflin, Boston.

ACKNOWLEDGEMENTS

The extracts from Commissioner T.R.H. Cole's report that appear in chapter 6 are from *The Loss of HMAS Sydney II: Vols 1, 2, 3,* 2009, copyright Commonwealth of Australia, reproduced by permission.

The quotations on pages 26, 44, 86, 110 are reproduced courtesy of Keith Shegog, from his book *Lost — But Not Forgotten: A Bitter Sweet Victory*, Single X Publications, Glenside, South Australia, 2002 and with permission of the individual copyright owners Thelma Gale, Sophie Jeffery, Margaret Morse, Leslie Michael Lawrence Blom, June Bickle and J.A. McLeod-Smith respectively. The quotation on page 64 was first published in Barbara Craill's book, *The Big Silence*, Hackham, 1997 and is reproduced with her permission. The publishers are grateful for the assistance of Keith Shegog in obtaining usage of this material.

Images and artifacts reproduced throughout the book are courtesy of the following: Australian National Archives; Australian War Memorial; J.S. Battye Library of West Australian History; Defence Science and Technology Organisation; Finding Sydney Foundation; Glenys McDonald Collection, and the donors to that collection Margaret Browne, the Crowle family, the Perryman family, Jim Lavender, the Cooper family; David Mearns; RAAF Historical Archives; Sea Power Centre—Australia; RSL Geraldton; West Australian Newspapers; Williamson and Associates. Acknowledgement is also due for images from the following Western Australian Museum collections and donors: Garry Baverstock, Burnsyde-Fox Collection, the Davis family, Gordon Ewers, Ros. Fielding, Elizabeth Goodwin, Maree Jenssen, the Meyer family, the Rolley family, W.H. (John) Ross Collection, Jochen Sachse, Ross Shardlow, H.J. Watson Collection. The specific details of sources are acknowledged below the captions for images.

Every effort has been made to locate copyright owners and to seek permission to reproduce images included in this book. In some cases this may not have been successful. The publisher would appreciate advice of ownership in these circumstances so that the correct attribution may be included in any future edition.

Comments on the draft manuscript were received from staff of the Commonwealth Department of Environment, Water, Heritage and the Arts, Ray Coffey, Ted Graham, Jeremy Green, Peter Hore, Kim Kirsner, Glenys McDonald, David Mearns, Wes Olson, John Perryman and Barbara Poniewierski. Editorial assistance was received from Ray Coffey and advice on images and captions from John Perryman.

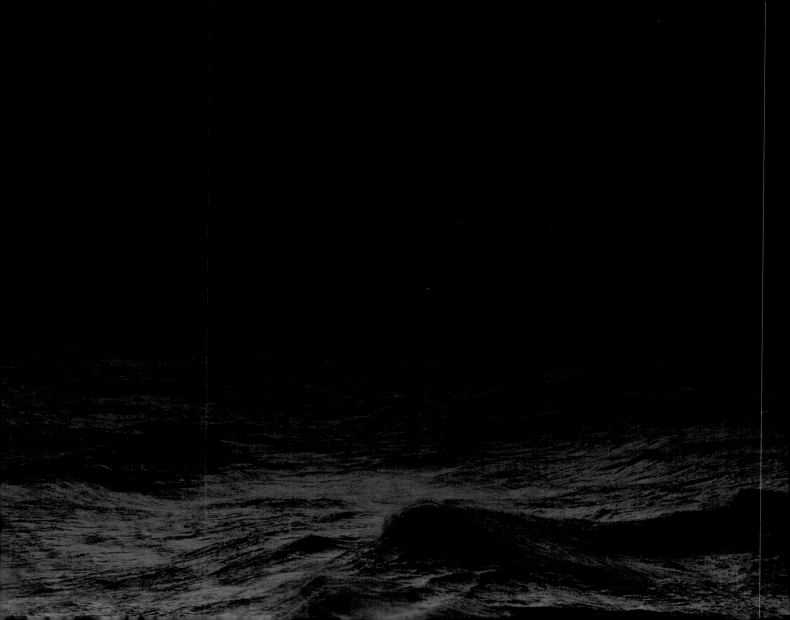

INDEX

LANG, John
LANG, William Hugh
LAWLER, Neil Charles
LAWSON, James Neil
LAXTON, Stewart Thomas
LAYCOCK, Royce Stanley
LEWIS, Ambrose Henry
LEWIS, Desmond Henry
LEWIS, Leslie Raymond
LILLYWHITE, Harry Edgar
LOCKARD, Terence Godfrey
LOVE, Snowden Edward
LOWENSTEIN, William
LOWRY, Frederick William
LYNCH, Stephen Maxwell
LYNE, Raymond Vivian
MACDONALD, Frank Leslie
MACKINNON, Murdo
MALES, Trevor
MANN, Keith Arthur
MANNING, Maurice
MARLEY, Sidney
MARSON, Albert Richard
MARTIN, Alan Douglas
MARTIN, James Hearle
MARTIN, Leslie Frank
MARTIN, Leslie James Frederick
MATHESON, Edward Austin John
MATHEWS, John William
MAXWELL, Ian Maxwell
MAYNARD, Thomas Francis
MAYO, Eric Elton
MCAULAY, Angas Campbell
MCAUSLAN, Arthur Robert
MCBAIN, Joseph Henry
MCCABE, Donald Wolsey
MCCABE, Ernest Victor
MCCALLUM, Duncan
MCCLAREN, Alfred Allan
MCCONNELL, Robert Nicol
MCCULLOCH, Sidney

MCCULLOUGH, Samuel James
MCDONALD, John Dennis
MCDOUGALL, Wallace
MCGOWAN, Thomas Henry
MCGREGOR, Donald Alexander
MCHAFFIE, Edward Hunter
MCKAY, Allan Murdoch
MCKECHNIE, Glen Morton
MCKENZIE, Donald James
MCKEOWN, Malachi James
MCLEAN, William Ernest
MCLEOD, Herbert Charles
MCLEOD-SMITH, Albert Fraser
MEDLEN, Lindsay James
MELANDRI, Percy Ernest Vincent
MENZIES, William
MILLER, George James
MILLER, James Douglas Haig
MILLER, Kenneth Roscoe
MILLER, Martin Patrick
MILLER, Robert Alfred
MILVERTON, Peter Frederick
MINNS, Leslie Charles
MITCHELL, Charles McGregor
MITCHELL, Francis Joseph
MOGLER, Richard Charles
MONTGOMERY, Clive Alexandra Craig
MORDAUNT, Francis Xavier
MORISEY, Ronald
MORPHETT, Merton James
MORRIS, Edgar Percy
MORRIS, Raymond Keith
MOULE, Albert
MUDFORD, Leslie Francis
MULHALL, John Dillon
MURDOCH, Raymond Charles
MURRAY, Malcolm
MUTCH, Hector MacDonald
MYERS, Henry William
NESBITT, Jackson
NEWMAN, Charles Albert

NICHOLLS, Malcolm Godfrey
NICHOLS, Francis Roy
NICHOLSON, Robert Wesley
NICOL, Thomas Enright
NOBLE, Charles Taylor
NOELL, Alfred John
NORBERY, Stephen William
NORMAN, Charles George James
NORMAN, Frederick William
NORTON, John Thomas Henry
NORTON, Montague Alfred Huxley
NORTON, William Frederick Cecil
NUGENT, Cyril James
NYAL, Leslie John
OAKFORD, Phillip James
O'BRIEN, Edward Bedford
OGILVIE, Laurence
OLIVER, Alan Henry
OPAS, Maurice
OWEN, William Albert
OWENS, Edward Harold
PALING, Dennis Ross
PARKES, Douglas Leon
PARR, George Frederick
PARTINGTON, Leslie Warburton
PASCOE, Percival Holman
PASTOORS, William Cecil
PATRICK, Charles William
PAUL, Stanley Robert
PAYNE, John Robert
PEAK, John McGhie
PEARCE, Eric Victor
PELHAM, Frederick Charles
PERGER, Frederick James
PERRYMAN, Richard Severn
PETERS, Maxwell Wesley
PETERSON, James Edward
PETERSON, Peter William
PHILLIPS, Frederick Ernest
PIKE, John William
PITT, William Harold

PLATT, Robert
POPLE, Alfred Herbert Wesley
POTTER, Alfred William
POTTER, Clyde Ashby
POWELL, Lyal Llewellyn
PRIKE, Joseph John
PRIMMER, John Foster Roy
PRITCHARD, Herbert Lloyd
PSAILA, Samuel
PULHAM, Edward George Montague
PURDON, Eric Thomas
PURKISS, Cecil Edward
PUTMAN, Albert Edward
QUILTY, John Edward
QUINN, George Frederick
RAMSAY, Ernest Wilson
RANFORD, John Irvine
RAY, Harold George
REDFEARNE, Charles Hugh
REDMOND, Eric Neville
REED, George Percival
REES, Robert John
REEVES, Ellis Leslie
REEVES, Raymond Henry
REID, Graham Roy
REILLY, James Bryan
REMFRY, Ernest John
REVILLE, Frederick William
RICARDO, John Layton
RICE, Desmond Maxwell
RICHARDS, Harold Nelson
RICHTER, Arthur John
RIDOUT, Robert Ernest
RILEY, Edwin Martin
RIPPEN, Adolf Heinrich Gerhard
RITERS, Edward
ROBERTS, Lyndon Irvine
ROBERTS, Ronald Charles
ROBERTSON, Michael John
ROBERTSON, Thomas Noel
ROBERTSON, William James